A Voice from the Past

'The most outspoken proponent of workers' control in Britain, Ken Coates, has seen the recent TUC proposals for industrial democracy ... as a "cautious step in the right direction"... The proposals of the Institute for Workers' Control at the time of the UCS occupations have more relevance than ever in today's recession.'

Gordon Brown, The Red Paper on Scotland, 1975

Workers' Control

Another world is possible

Arguments from the
Institute for Workers' Control

By

Ken Coates

With introductory contributions by
Derek Simpson & Tony Woodley

SPOKESMAN
for
SOCIALIST RENEWAL

First published in 2003 by
Spokesman
Russell House, Bulwell Lane
Nottingham
NG6 0BT
Phone 0115 970 8318.   Fax 0115 942 0433.
e-mail elfeuro@compuserve.com
www.spokesmanbooks.com

ISBN 0 85124 682 6

A CIP Catalogue is available from the British Library.

Printed by the Russell Press Ltd (phone 0115 978 4505).

Contents

Introductory Note

The Institute for Workers' Control was formed in 1968 with the blessing of Hugh Scanlon and Jack Jones, leaders of the Engineers and Transport workers respectively. For a number of years the IWC was able to organise widespread discussions on all aspects of industrial democracy, and published dozens of pamphlets and books which helped to popularise the idea. Its ideas found their way into the TUC through education courses, and into the machinery of collective bargaining, as they were taken up and developed by workers' representatives.

Under Thatcher, with mass unemployment, anti-union laws and the development of a defensive style of trade unionism, notions of workers' control were put on the backburner. But they remain as relevant as ever, even if the circumstances in which they will henceforward find application are markedly different.

This book is a significant contribution to the ongoing discussion around issues of workers' control. We believe that this selection of writings will assist in the huge tasks facing us today, namely expanding trade union organisation, strengthening collective bargaining, and reasserting and developing workers' control over their lives and industry.

Jeremy Dear	*National Union of Journalists*
Andy Gilchrist	*Fire Brigades Union*
Billy Hayes	*Communication Workers' Union*
Joe Marino	*Bakers, Food & Allied Workers' Union*
Mick Rix	*Associated Society of Locomotive Engineers & Firemen*
Mark Serwotka	*Public & Commercial Services Union*
Tony Woodley	*Transport & General Workers' Union*

Foreword I
Workers' Control
by Derek Simpson
General Secretary Amicus – AEEU

The Institute for Workers' Control played an important role in formulating the industrial strategy of the labour and trades union movement in the 60s and 70s, and the lessons learnt have a striking relevance to the challenges facing the trade union movement in today's global economy. Ken Coates' *Workers' Control* provides an intellectual framework for the restoration of effective industrial democracy in the 21st century.

Today we are faced with the legacy of the sweetheart deals entered into in the 80s and 90s. As we know, the Thatcher Government was determined to destroy trade unions and, at the time, it was espoused that any agreement was better than none at all. The need to attract inward investment to Britain was used as an apology for abandoning fundamental elements of trade union agreements.

Many of these sweetheart deals do not recognise the role of shop stewards nor the right of the trade union to negotiate over pay on behalf of the staff. We have the farcical situation of shop stewards denied time off for trade union duties under a single union agreement, no access to staff in order to recruit and, most ridiculous of all, pay negotiations conducted with a company appointed staff council with no role for the union. The reps at companies covered by these agreements have complained of years of frustration and alienation.

The current Government's fairness at work agenda is unfinished business, and the UK still has the most restrictive laws on trade unions in the western world. The collective bargaining framework must be based on the understanding that the unions' legitimate role is to act to protect their members' interests; only then can we build meaningful industrial partnership with employers. This will only be achieved when backed by a framework of employment law that requires employers to come to the bargaining table.

Foreword II

Mandate for Change

by Tony Woodley

General Secretary Transport & General Workers' Union

The Transport and General Workers' Union held an election during the year 2003, to find a successor to Sir Bill Morris, who is retiring from the general secretaryship.

The new leader is Tony Woodley. There follows an excerpt from his inaugural speech to the Union's Biennial Delegate Conference in Brighton.

It sums up the characteristics which ensured his election, and at the same time, captures the character of the man. But it also represents a clear statement of the traditions of the Union, and of those values which have marked it out as a special influence in the British Labour Movement.

The Transport and General Workers' Union has a lifelong association with the ideals of workers' control, beautifully captured in this statement.

Let me spell out to you where I am coming from. I stood for election using the slogan of 'vote for change and make a difference'.

This was more than a slogan, it was a mandate for change – for real change in the way the T&G does its business. Not ill-thought out change for change's sake, but a reorientation in our thinking, our outlook and our attitudes.

But we must start with our culture. We are not a business. We must be business-like and professional in the way that we conduct ourselves, but we are not a business – we are a trade union, an organisation of Officers and Staff not master and servants. The language of business, ie chief executive, directors, managers, supervisors, is inappropriate for our union.

Many of our members already believe that we are too close to the bosses without us sounding, dressing talking and acting like them – this must change. We are a team whose wages are paid for by the members, working together for the members. And only for the members – no other interest.

But real change must start at the sharp end – in the workplace. Every day's news underlines how important that is. We live in a society where workers can be sacked by text message. Where unscrupulous employers close down factories here because it is quicker, cheaper and easier to sack British workers than those elsewhere in Europe. Where poverty pay remains rife, and women and black people are second-class citizens at work. We live in a world where there is too often a race to the bottom in terms and conditions for workers, where the bad employer is able to undercut the good. A world of pensions robbery for those at the bottom and unbridled fat cat greed at the top.

And we have to recognise it – a society where the trade union movement has been able to do too little to help those who need us most.

Over the last year I have met tens of thousands of T&G members around the country. It has been an exhilarating experience – but also at times a sobering, even a depressing, one. How many times have I heard workers say, 'why isn't the union doing anything for us?' Even, 'what is the point in the union?' And if those who are already our members are saying that, we can only imagine what the attitude is among those millions who aren't in unions.

Why? Because we have taken our eye off the ball, because, we are sometimes seen as too close to the gaffer, because we are not delivering satisfaction at the sharp end, in the workplace, we have become almost irrelevant to our members.

That is why we must refocus our time, money and effort on the workplace and industrial priorities of the union, on the T&G becoming once more a 'fighting back union'.

Some people may misinterpret that as a permanent call to arms, or a programme of endless strikes. That is not the case. What I mean is a T&G that:

- Never lets an injustice in the workplace go by without challenging it.
- Encourages, rather than damps down, the aspirations of working people.
- When a problem arises, always meets the members before we meet the governor.
- And, if our members decide they need to fight to secure improvements to pay and conditions, equality, or to save their jobs, gets right behind them one hundred and ten per cent and FIGHTS TO WIN.

10

That philosophy has served me well and I don't intend to change my approach now. That is why I have said loud and clear that social partnership is not the way forward for working people. Of course, I don't mean that we stop negotiating, that we stop reaching pragmatic agreements with employers, that we don't have constructive engagement, or that we stop respecting companies that respect their own workforce and their unions.

But it does mean ending the situation where we look at a company's business plan and demands before we look at our own member's needs and demands. How many times do you hear the members say: 'why are you ramming ballots down our throats – we've had one and we have told you, the answer's NO – get out and do better'? How many times have we found imaginative ways to pressurise you to vote yes? This behaviour will stop.

We must put aside the illusion that if we all just pull our socks up and work harder, the employer will look after us: I have never met a generous employer in my life. Look around you; every industrial community in this country has reminders in closed factories and derelict industrial areas, communities destroyed as corporate greed takes its toll. Shareholder value being the only value whilst the stakeholders, you our members, pay the price with lost jobs. Fighting back means standing up, and being seen to stand up for the interests of our members, no matter whose cage gets rattled in the process.

I am not interested in being loved by Labour ministers because I sell members short. I will gain respect as they and others understand – it is 'members first' no matter who is getting in the way. And I believe that standing up for our members today is the surest way to win the members of tomorrow – to attract the millions of unorganised workers in Britain into the T&G.

Let me now turn to the issue of organisation. We all know that we need a bigger T&G – millions out there need it, and our existing membership can only profit from being part of a stronger organisation. Size matters politically and industrially.

And let me pay tribute here to the many members of our union who are, day in and day out, putting such efforts into recruitment and building the T&G. But we all know it has not been enough. We all know the plans; the strategies, the seminars and the conferences have

11

not stopped the decline. We now need a new approach, new energy, a new vision and resources at the front line, coupled with real commitment from the very top of the T&G to grow the union.

My message is simple: The T&G is back. It will be back in the communities we have abandoned, as fast as resources can permit. And I will be asking regions to identify towns where a case can be made for a new, physical T&G presence.

Let me make one thing clear, contrary to my critics' pronouncements, I will not bankrupt the Union. The union's finances are safe in my hands. We will, however, target and pilot new offices in line with indisputable growth opportunities. My critics will also be somewhat surprised by the visionary and imaginative ways in which we will achieve our goals.

But I make this point. You don't need £3 million offices like some monument to Ceausescu on the smartest docksides and quaysides, which are completely inaccessible to members, to recruit £4.50 poorly paid workers – we just need to be there when they need us. In communities, part of communities.

We will be back in the workplaces where the employer does not want us. I renew my promise here, to build separate specialist organising teams in the regions to put the T&G on the doorstep and in the face of every anti-union employer in the country. And to work for 100% membership in our already organised workplaces.

I visited 91 factories and workplaces during the recent election, none were fully unionised, far from it. We must say no to no go areas for recruitment.

And we will be back in the mergers market. I know that mergers do not on their own make an extra trade unionist. But I also know that a stronger union can recruit more readily, can make better use of resources and can eliminate that wasteful competition between unions which only benefits management.

So I pledge to start, in fact we have already started, aggressively seeking mergers which make industrial sense for the T&G, and which can ensure that our great democratic traditions are respected.

When this parliament of our Union next meets, I am confident that we can be representing an expanding T&G, not a contracting one, and that we will have broken the psychology of decline for good.

I, like I am sure all of you here, reject the false division between industrial work and political activity which some pundits try to create. They say it is all right for trade unions to deal with workplace matters, but that it is almost an impertinence to speak about politics. If you do, you risk being called a 'wrecker' by the great and the good. Well, I've been called nicer things, but worse things too. Let me make it clear to the hard of understanding – the T&G has been involved in politics from its foundation, and will always be so. That is for two good reasons. First, so many of the problems we face at work can be made better – or worse – by what is done or not done in parliament. Second, working people have a collective vision not just of better working lives, but also of better lives in their communities and around the world. As a great democratic working class organisation, the T&G will always hold true to that vision.

So I want to take this opportunity to make it clear where I stand on the political questions facing this union. We must start by facing the reality of the bitter disappointment that working men and women throughout the country feel towards this government.

I don't have selective amnesia about how bad it was under a Tory administration, but for a Labour Government, or anyone else, six years in to say 'remember the Tories and therefore be happy with what you've got' is unacceptable.

I ask the question:

- Why is this the first Labour Government in our history under which the gap between rich and poor has grown?
- Why is this the first Labour Government in our history to leave on the statute book anti-union laws, illegal laws, placed there by the Tories, in violation of ILO standards?
- Why are Friction Dynamics workers, unfairly sacked after 8 weeks, not legally entitled to go back to their jobs?
- Why is this the first Labour Government in our history which has sought to extend privatisation, rather than advance the public sector?
- Why is this the first Labour Government in our history to do nothing – nothing – to protect working class communities from the devastation of redundancies and closures?
- And why is this the first Labour Government in our history to abandon the principles of peace and international law and line up instead with a reckless, aggressive reactionary US administration?

Perhaps we are part of the answer to that question. Perhaps it is because the trade union movement has not been firm enough and early enough in drawing a line in the sand.

Let me put that right here today. The days of New Labour are now numbered. Working people want something different.

I say it is time to reclaim our Party. Not walk away from it as a few on the fringes would argue, but reclaim it for the values of working class men and women, the values of socialism.

We cannot do it alone. But I am prepared to work with our brothers and sisters in other trade unions to put the Labour back in our Party. That means an end to privatisation, an end to anti-union laws, an end to pandering to big business, and an end to wars of aggression. It also means taking another look at the Party's democracy, at opening up the structures so policy is no longer handed down from the top with no room to challenge or question it, but built up from the bottom, reflecting the experiences of our people. If we can make that change in our Party we will not just be doing a favour to T&G members or trade unionists, but to democracy as a whole. Apathy and disillusionment in our political system is spreading, and sinister forces are working to take advantage of that – filling the gap of frustrated, disillusioned and disappointed Labour– voting people.

Let me say here, that this Union will be in the forefront of fighting against the BNP and the poison it represents in any community where it raises its head. And I can also make it clear that there will never be any place for fascists or racists within the ranks of the T&G. Where we find them, we will root them out, and we will drive them out.

Many other challenges face us. We cannot relax for a moment in our fight for genuine equality in our Union, at work and in society as a whole. We have made progress, but not so much that we can allow ourselves a moment's complacency. I am not happy that there are only three women among our national officials, and only one black person once Bill Morris retires. If that is still the position in a few year's time, never mind five or ten, I will have failed. Let's get equality out of the conferences, out of the composites and into our daily lives.

Nor can we continue to allow ourselves the luxury of thinking that our practical tasks stop at Dover. Capital is global. While Labour remains local, we will too often be on the back foot against the Trans-

National Corporations. Internationalism is no longer just a matter of solidarity, important though that is. It is a matter of finding ways of working with our brothers and sisters in other lands which can actually level up the playing field with global big business and end the situation where workers in one land can be used to undercut workers in others. There is no more important task for the future.

I would like to return to the theme I started with. I want to lead a united Union. I know that you all want to work and be active in a united Union. I want my team to be 850,000-strong – as a start!

I do not stand before you as someone who has all the answers. I believe I am asking the right questions, the ones our members are themselves asking. Only together do we have any chance of finding the right solutions.

I am conscious that I am standing in the shoes of giants – of Bevin, Cousins and Jack Jones. Alone, I cannot hope to fill them. Together, we can do more than that – we can stride forward to new victories for working people.

I stand here as your servant. Your decisions will be my only guide in my new responsibilities.

I am not here for patronage or a pay rise.

I am not here for a quiet life.

I am here to help this great Union realise in the twenty-first century, the vision that made us strong in the twentieth. Of justice and decency for working people in a socialist Britain and a peaceful world. With your help, with your support we can make it happen, we can make that difference.

Preface

This book is called *Workers' Control*, because of its subject matter and its provenance. It contains a small selection of those of my writings which were generated during campaigns initiated by the Institute for Workers' Control. This was formally launched in 1968, but was the subject of rather a long preparation, involving five national conferences from 1963 onwards. The Institute was launched at the sixth conference. Before that, academics, trade union activists and leaders, writers and adult educationalists had met at fairly regular intervals to consider how to advance industrial democracy, and widen the argument in its support. Most of these people came from the political left, but not all. There was a strong Young Liberal input from some of the earliest conferences, and older members soon joined in. But the debate inside the Labour Party inevitably spilled over into the emerging workers' control movement, because of its evident relevance.

During these years the Labour Party was itself undergoing a somewhat painful evolution even while it formed the Government, to say nothing of its periods in opposition. By contrast, the trade unions were embarked upon a steady growth of membership and influence. The post-war Labour Government had carried through an extensive programme of nationalisation, which had brought up to a fifth of the economy into one or another form of public ownership. Coal, gas, electricity, railways, road haulage, airlines and steel were all brought into this net. The predominant mode of organisation which was chosen was the public corporation, broadly modelled on the pattern established by Herbert Morrison between the wars in London Transport. Some nine hundred private mines, many of them ramshackle, were reorganised by the National Coal Board, into a very much more efficient productive ensemble. Overall, the post-war years registered considerable gains in industrial efficiency, in large part because of the reorganisations which were facilitated by nationalisation. Public pricing policies could also furnish hidden subsidies to the private sector, doubtless improving its competitive power.

16

At the same time, the Attlee administration carried through a revolution in the organisation of the social services, most notably in the creation of the National Health Service, reforms in education, and the enactment of many of the Beveridge recommendations for social insurance. These major changes not only laid the foundations of the subsequent Welfare State, but facilitated a great expansion of trade union organisation, opening up important democratic possibilities.

These were not all seized, however. Whatever it did for production statistics, nationalisation quickly disabused its workforces of whatever hope they may have nurtured for greater democratic influence over their jobs. One democratic gain was beyond question: full employment gave a measure of genuine economic power to the workforce. But beyond this, Morrisonian nationalisation fell far short of the promise of the Labour Party's aim (in Clause IV, item 4 of its Constitution):

> 'to secure for the workers by hand or by brain the full fruits of their industry and the most equitable distribution thereof that may be possible upon the basis of the common ownership of the means of production, distribution, and exchange, *and the best obtainable system of popular administration and control of each industry or service.*'

Drawing the balance sheet, Hugh Scanlon, the engineers' leader, was later to warn that

> 'with nationalisation, workers must not be made to feel, as they certainly do at present, that there is only a political change while there remains an industrial status quo. Fundamentally, the aim within public ownership is the wearing down of sides in industry, with no "superiors" or "inferiors" but only differences and functions based on knowledge and ability. Only through public ownership could there be this real will to co-operate.'

Much of the argument within the Institute for Workers' Control originally involved different proposals for the administration of public enterprise. Over the preceding half century, in the railways, the mines, the Post Office, and other industries, there had been extensive debate about the best forms of democratic organisation open to publicly owned industries and services, and the movement of the 1960s dug deep into those old trade union debates about guild socialism, industrial unionism, syndicalism, and other proposals for democratic reform. New proposals were launched for instance by steel workers, busmen, dockers and mine workers. The common denominator of all

17

these proposals, old and new, involved the understanding that public ownership was not enough, and that democracy was the necessary key to unlock the arbitrary power of property.

In this sense, the workers' control movement from its foundation offered a new interpretation of the Labour Party's conventional doctrines.

But if this argument began in the public sector of the economy, it certainly could not be confined within that sector. With trade union growth, workers' control came to seem a more and more natural response to problems of arbitrary power through the entire economy and society. The idea of workers' control became an invitation to extend democratic forms widely across society, and encourage democratic initiatives.

As they grew in strength through the 1960s, the trade unions became more and more aware of the need for a complete reform of industrial structures. As they built their representative capacity, they found themselves able to arrive at informed opinions on a wide range of matters from the consideration of which they had previously been excluded. They began to feel the need to be able to bargain constructively about the direction of the enterprise, rather than simply to respond negatively about the distribution of rewards.

Sustained by relatively full employment, we saw a growing interest in the question of industrial democracy, and the development of a wide variety of proposals to admit employees into the processes of management. The spectrum of debate was wide. At one edge, an almost infinite variety of proposals for different degrees of workers' control was canvassed. At the other edge, generations of personnel managers debated the improvement of procedures for consultation. But reform was almost supernaturally difficult.

The formal debate ranged the Trade Union Congress on the side of a cluster of proposals which were ultimately to be refined into the Bullock Report on Industrial Democracy. The Labour Government prevaricated. The implementation of Bullock, which received very wide support both in the trade unions and in the Labour Party at large, was put in the hands of a Cabinet Committee which dithered and procrastinated with rare skill. In the end, we got not Bullock, but the Winter of Discontent.

So it was that the offer of a constructive role for trade unions in all the processes of industrial innovation and management was spiked. With the election of Mrs. Thatcher, exclusion followed exclusion, as unions were eliminated from one Governmental process after another. New laws were introduced to restrict their every movement. From time to time, the legislative process of rolling back the unions was interrupted by set-piece industrial battles of great brutality and ruthlessness. The worst of these, the miners' strike of 1984, was provoked and managed by the Government with all the assiduity it had previously shown in the reconquest of the Falkland Islands.

These were to be the Thatcher years, in which unemployment combined with legislative intervention to weaken trade union powers. From this time on, the argument about workers' control became less urgent and more academic, as trade unions necessarily became preoccupied with the raw problems of survival in a hostile world.

There was a significant area of interest in industrial democracy, which followed the development of industrial relations policies in Europe, the spread of European works councils, and the growth of co-operation between European national trade union centres. These developments are not the subject of this book which nonetheless may have some relevance to unions which now reach towards their continental colleagues, across a bewildering history of different movements and industrial relations systems.

The British Labour leadership sought to wipe the slate clean when it annulled Clause IV of the Party's Constitution. But Clause IV continues to haunt us, since its absence merely celebrates the victory of neo-liberalism over Labour's old ideals. Present day arguments about the unbridled appetites of fat cats are nothing but an assertion of the untrammelled power of property to determine rewards.

Workers' control always took its beginnings from the most elementary forms of collective bargaining, which have still to be painstakingly restored in Britain. But the struggle for industrial democracy is no less relevant because it has counted more defeats than are comfortable, during recent years. Many of its victories are to come, but not the least of them is the present victory, which sees us greeting a veritable rebirth of the trade union spirit, even as the adversary has closed its grip on some of the cardinal institutions of political labour.

1

From a Mob to a Movement

Throughout the late '80s, I was privileged to work alongside Tony Topham in the research and writing of the first volume of The History of the Transport and General Workers' Union. *We had been given powerful encouragement by the Union's General Secretary, Ron Todd, who had ensured that we had the most complete access to the Union's archives, whilst guaranteeing the widest freedom in the composition of the work itself.*

The formation of the Union was a particularly significant moment in the development of the movement for workers' control in Great Britain. We were able to trace the influence of the pioneers who were nourished by the syndicalist movement, the ideas of industrial unionism, guild socialism and industrial democracy. Some were already widely known, as were Tom Mann, Ben Tillett, Ernest Bevin and James Larkin. Others had been unjustly forgotten, and we found amongst the Union's crumbling records, pages of incredible freshness, containing some of the exciting arguments of Bob Williams, who played a heroic role in the extension of trade unionism among unskilled workers, especially in the transport industry.

At last the book was published in May 1991 by Basil Blackwell. It occupied two stout volumes, and we dedicated it to:

'The memory of the pioneers, who dreamed of One Big Union, and to the success of their heirs, the members of the Transport and General Workers' Union.'

One big union still eludes us, but the dream was directly related to the goal of industrial democracy, seeking, as it did, to overcome sectionalism in the separate trade unions, and emphasise the common interests of the working class movement as a whole.

In June 1991, the Union's Midlands Region sponsored a seminar with the Department of Adult Education at Nottingham University, which brought together active shop stewards and branch officials, together with full-time officers representing both the East and West Midlands. Jim Hunt, the Regional Secretary, was kind enough to refer to our joint role as what he called 'the moving spirits of the Institute for Workers' Control, which did a lot of pioneering work "for the past twenty or thirty years" on the question of industrial democracy'.

The seminar began with a presentation by Tony Topham called Unity in Diversity, *which explained how the General Union tackled the abiding problems of sectionalism, and encouraged the widest possible representative cover.*

My lecture focused on the remarkable transformation of the chaotic and struggling mass of poor people into the beginnings of a disciplined and proud trade union movement.

It seems worthwhile to include it in this account of some of the ideas of the movement for workers' control, because it explains the material origins of a key sector of trade unionism, and the seedbed of the ideas which it subsequently developed.

Both essays were published in a single pamphlet with the title One Big Union, *which we gave a subtitle: 'Founding the Transport and General Workers' Union: the Birth of the Modern Labour Movement'.*

Unfortunately the two original hardback volumes of the history are now out of print: but a paperback version, published under the title The Making of the Labour Movement *does exist, and is obtainable from Spokesman Books.*

Why bother with history? Perhaps the best way to explain is to try to draw for you a picture of what the allegedly unskilled workers, who gave us our subject matter, were like. How did they live, in the forgotten corners of Victorian Britain?

The fact of the matter is that in all British industrial towns, and above all, in the port cities, life was hell for the poorest people. It was calculated by sociologists, at the end of the century, that approximately one-third of the population of London was living in poverty, and by poverty they did not mean what modern sociologists mean. They meant dire and suffocating squalor. Poverty meant tenements in which sometimes five or ten people lived in one room. It meant courtyards where the water supply, such as it was, was shared between many such households. It meant privies that had to be emptied by the night soil man. London, for instance, in the last days at the end of nineteenth century Britain, had a whole tract of housing in the East End which was, as William Blake and Cobbett used to say in earlier days, 'a wen'. I am reminded of modern China when I look at those discrepancies between wealth and poverty. The West End, home of the lords of the earth, the owners of empire, people of unparalleled riches and ostentation, lay on one side. On the other was the East End crawling with vice, terrified by Jack the Ripper, a horrendous stew.

And what happened in those straitened circumstances? People normally have a certain capacity for supporting one another. People can normally be kindly, friendly and helpful, and there was, among these particular people, every need for all those resources of solidarity and decency, which the poorest of them could muster. But also, when one is competing for life, there are many instincts which pit people against each other. It can be a brutal struggle, each against all, for survival of those who are miscalled the fittest, which often means survival of the less conscientious and the least moral in the deprived population. All these things were mixed together, base and pure; mean, and generous to a fault.

We do not try to give you an idealised picture. Instead we try to recover the feel of those communities. The docks grew up in cities which had exploded in size, because the rail networks were decanting people into these vital areas at a rate far faster than the cities themselves could grow to assimilate them. Many or most of the people who were sucked into these growing urban areas were agricultural people. I have always thought it is a libel to say that such people were unskilled, but they had skills from a previous age. That is why so many of them became carters, because they knew about horses. Many others became dockers: many swapped roles, and many of the country people who did not actually migrate would find themselves drawn into the town after the harvest was in, which was when unemployment hit the agricultural labourers. Nearly always the docks had far more people wanting to work than could normally be given work. There were just rare moments when the weather was right, when the winds were right, when the demand was right, when the ships lined up to unload, that you could have something which fleetingly resembled full employment. Normally this was not so.

Work was organised quite differently in such places from the orderly rhythms we came to expect later in the car factories, which are so well understood and well remembered in the Midlands. The industrial discipline of this population that we are talking about hardly existed. People had come from the land, they had not become inured to the routine of the hooter and the clock, still less the drill of time study and careful managerial control. They queued up outside the dock gates and fought to get in. The foreman picked the fittest and set them on. The rest were sent away. They would go hungry.

So what are we talking about? Why have I gone into all this? I have gone into it because I want you to understand that everything that we take for granted today about trade unions was still unformed, unfixed: everything. We take for granted that there are and have always been working class people. But in a sense, in those days, these were not such working class people. Then, in the docks, there was a mob, when it all got together: and when it was not together there were tens of thousands of miserable individuals normally ground down into isolation, loneliness and poverty. Yet somehow or other those same people became a collective which was not a mob, no longer a bunch of social atoms either. They became something which today everybody assumes has always been with us, an independent-minded working class, with a self-confident working class movement. Banding those previously forlorn people together was actually the major breakthrough which created modern British democracy.

I know in school we were told it all started with the Magna Carta, 1215 and I don't know what. But actually at the time we are speaking about, the very large majority of British people had no say whatever about who were to become the politicians who might lead them. All women lacked the vote, but very large numbers of men also lacked the vote. There had been a big electoral reform in 1884, and the working class electorate had been increased. But it depended on various complex qualifications, according to household tenure, and there was the additional problem that middle class people commonly had two votes, because they could vote where they lived, and they could also vote where they held business property. That meant that you could not just take the electorate and do the sums and work out what the entitlement to political involvement was. And that is why, in the words of the old song,

'Every little Briton who's ever born alive,
is either a little Liberal or a little Conservative.'

The prosperous classes monopolised the vote. When you shared a tenement room in East London with all those other families, you lived in a world where things like voting could hardly be imagined.

And then suddenly, something happens. We see the outcast people associating themselves. Ben Tillett is one of the great heroes in this story, and what Ben Tillett says he did is very revealing. When he started work on the docks, having been a seaman, he took upon himself a stigma which made it impossible to confess where he was actually employed. Outside his work, when he was mixing in 'society', he would try to conceal what his job was. People who were doing his job were universally described as 'dock rats'. Ben Tillett claimed that he himself was the man who invented the word 'docker', which description marked a new beginning. It gave both self-repect and, yes, status to the job. But why were they seen, and why did they see themselves, as 'dock rats'? Because in order to get work, in attending the call-on, which was the selection of the fittest men to work those ships that were available for working, the men had, quite normally, to fight each other to be chosen. It was a raw, physical battle. There were innumerable descriptions of it, including lots by sociologists who began to visit and report at the time. It was a war. People's coats (and, said Tillett, sometimes even their ears) were torn off in the struggle to get to the gate and earn the pittance which was the difference between starvation – there was no Welfare State – and a meagre livelihood. Sometimes men would be injured and maimed in the battle. All sorts of attempts were made to organise these people.

At the end of the 1880s, however, this whole submerged population exploded in a great rage of rebellion. It was started by the matchgirls who worked in Bryant and Mays' factory in Bow. They rebelled because they were levied a penny a week contribution, a compulsory tax put on them by the employer, an important Liberal, who demonstrated his Party loyalty by building a statue of Gladstone, at the girls' expense, outside the factory. The girls were enraged by this, and in fact they mutinied when the statue was unveiled. There was a mob scene, when the girls threw themselves on the statue, and actually it got covered in blood where they had been beating it with their bare hands. So enraged were they all about the forced deduction of money to sustain a political cause which, they felt, had nothing to do with them. And yet it surely did have something to do with them, because they were the most exploited and suffocated group of people that you could ever meet. We have a picture of them. Little waifs, they were, and they got all kinds of industrial diseases, including the dreadful malady, 'phossy jaw', from the phosphorus used in the matches they made. This melts the bones. One of these children appeared in the House of Commons when the final strike broke out, and took her headscarf off, to the astonishment of the MPs, because all her hair had fallen out. Actually, that was the least of the problems, and many worse things than that happened. But that glimpse of hell so shattered the MPs that they all declared themselves in support of the matchgirls. And when the East End of London was hit by this unlikely strike, it caused a tremendous amount of public concern. The truth about poverty and exploitation became momentarily visible to more comfortable people.

That lit a fire which spread out, so that there was a huge conflagration among, first, the gasworkers, and then, the dockers. This was the movement which generated the great dock strike of 1889.

That dock strike was a fantastic event. It mobilised a hundred thousand people of East London, the poorest people not only on the docks, but all around them. They paraded through London day after day after day, and as they made their processions their grievances were paraded in the press. We had, in 1889, just entered the beginning of the age of the modern popular press, so those grievances presented themselves all over the country. So, indeed, did their rebellion. Suddenly you could see the poorest of the nation marching together and insisting that their complaints should be heard. In this way, all over the country, the dock strike was seen as a flame of rage and indignation, and of protest and hope. And now what did that do?

Well, you know that in history there are many examples of similar outbreaks, in which oppressed people have risen up and asserted themselves: and there are many of these examples – I could cite the history of some of the great strikes of the American labour movement, when after a year had gone by you could go back to see where that rebellion had been and find not a trace left of it. Nothing. People had vented their anger and then sunk back into quiescence.

But what the London dockers did was more than rebel. They set out to create a union and to demand negotiations between the dockers and the port employers. A variety of other material demands were concerned. But all of them involved a new and central demand for recognition.

Recognition is the magic word. Its achievement, over time, did not just bring about collective bargaining: it also brought with it modern democracy. And that is why we must ask, what does recognition mean? There you had among the dock employers the most disreputable bunch of old feudal magnates that ever there was. They really were money-grubbing, grasping, backward-looking monsters. Against this grouping, the dockers' union, with the help of the Catholic Church in the person of Cardinal Manning, with the help of parts of the Liberal establishment, and with the help of the liberal press, notably the evening paper in London, *The Star,* managed to create such a pressure that even these, the most backward employers in the land, were compelled to negotiate. They were compelled to recognise that these workmen were no longer individual 'dock rats'. Now they were the Dockers' Union. You see what that means: first of all, it means the dockers had won their claims; secondly, it means the dockers could build their organisation; thirdly, and this is the key question, it means that the dockers could recognise their own unity, their community of interest, through its reflection in the eyes of their enemy. He *recognised* them. Their basic wage and conditions, then, came to depend upon their adversary's recognition that they had been agreed, with the union.

So the men were a unity. I think that is a core element in the creation of modern democracy, because it meant that the poor, once they got the idea of union into their heads, even if the recognition was later taken away, had already experienced what was to become crucial to them: the knowledge that their individual strength would inevitably be the greater when they belonged to a collective in which they had confidence and trust. That is the basis upon which they began to organise, not only collective bargaining in industry, but the long and difficult process which led to political representation.

Of course political action became necessary because the people who were 'recognised' were a minority of the great population outside, clamouring for work. Although you could try to organise similar recognition for that wider population, and perhaps win many successes, it was a bit like baling out the ocean with a spoon. To make a substantial change, extending recognition to all who needed it, you had to get political representation and you had to get the vote. But to use that vote you had also to win a second recognition, expressing your own special political interests in distinction to those of the existing parties, representing the comfortable classes.

It wasn't an accident that the girls in Bryant and May rebelled about the statue of Gladstone. The Liberal employers were among the most persistent of all in exploiting the un-unionised labour forces and in driving down conditions. The same thing was the case in Brunner Mond, the forerunners of ICI; in one of the chapters of *The Making of the Labour Movement* we describe how Tom Mann became involved in a big effort to impose shorter hours and safe conditions in that enterprise. He had to adopt an alias, and smuggle himself into employment, so keen were these employers to keep out unions and all who might advance them.

Voting Liberal, then, which was what such working class voters as there were were most commonly wont to do, was not going to advance their interests at work, because the same Liberals who stood on the hustings promising all kinds of benevolence were also the big employers who resisted unions. So there grew up a campaign for separate labour representation. And you see, recognition, representation, these are all parts of the creation of an identity. It wasn't already there: it had to be made, it had to be built.

Of course, what happened was that the dock strike led directly to the election of the first really independent Labour MP, Keir Hardie, Member for West Ham, and also to the election of John Burns, who had played a key role in 1889, and of Havelock Wilson, the Seamen's leader. These political events arose directly from the organisation of the dockers and the surrounding transport and general workers, the gas workers, the people involved as carters and all the rest of them.

In turn, organisation led directly into local government representation, with the winning of Labour voices on the new local councils, first of all in the London area and then further afield. When Keir Hardie was elected, although he was not a docker, he became the political representative of the dockers' new unionism, and he was directly supported by the leaders of that process. Keir Hardie was elected three years after the great dock strike.

The year after that, in 1893, there met the first conference of the Independent Labour Party (ILP). It was called in Bradford. Who was the Parliamentary candidate of the ILP in Bradford? Who but our old friend Ben Tillett! Very soon afterwards, Tom Mann was selected as the Independent Labour candidate in Halifax.

When you ask why, what you find is that in Bradford, too, they had an immense strike, the Manningham Mills dispute. It had been caused by contraction in the textile industry resulting from trade protection in the United States. That strike itself created an enormous popular unity and rebellion in Bradford, but the Bradford people, including their leaders, looked towards the dockers' leaders, because those dockers' leaders had been advertised all over the country as near miracle-workers. These, after all, were the people who had turned the people of the East End from a lethargic and dispersed mass of individuals into a united fighting force. So, send for Ben Tillett, send for Tom Mann! And up they came to Yorkshire. Who better to choose as parliamentary candidates? But we should notice that they, too, were the people who sharpened the argument so that the ILP was actually begun, and within one year, Tom Mann, who was the dockers' President, had also become the General Secretary of the ILP.

It was the struggle of these same leaders of the transport workers which persuaded the TUC itself to go for shorter working hours by law, in the campaign for the legal eight hour day. This we still have not won. But it was these leaders who prepared the ground for the formation of the political Labour Party, the party we know today, and a key issue in that argument was that of working time. Shorter hours by law were not what Liberal employers wanted. So in Parliament they voted against. Everyone could then see what limits there were to liberal philanthropy.

At the turn of the century, it was the Liverpool dockers' leader, James Sexton, and the London dockers' leader, Ben Tillett, who joined forces with the railwaymen's union to put down proposals at the TUC in 1899, ten years after the story began, to convene the conference which founded the Labour Party. Those three organisations met to composite their separate resolutions into a joint motion, under the chairmanship of Keir Hardie. This was then carried through the Trades Union Congress (TUC), so that the conference that called the Labour Party into being was two-thirds the responsibility of the Transport and General Workers' forerunners, and one-third the responsibility of their allies in what later became the National Union of Railwaymen (NUR).

Now why? The answer is that this political struggle was absolutely essential for the poorest people, because they lacked the monopoly position of skilled workers. They could not trade on their scarcity. Instead they had to secure some political intervention to make space for recognition.

Recognition was reinforced by government intervention, by the government holding the ring in industrial relations between the two sides. The government indeed made very tentative interventions in this process throughout the first part of this century. As time wore on, it made more and more strong appearances, culminating in a rush of government actions establishing a powerful presence during the First World War. But each intervention reinforced recognition, and therefore reinforced the sense of identity that workers got from seeing their unity reflected in the adversary's eyes. That is what made possible what happened after the First World War, the displacement of the Liberal Party by a Labour opposition led by Ramsay MacDonald.

None of that would have happened if there had been no successful move to organise the so-called unskilled workers. And all of it was a direct result of what? Of the inventive skills of these same dispossessed people.

The transport workers did not follow lamely behind the skilled workers, the aristocrats of labour. At the beginning of the trade union story, there were some skilled workers' unions in which you would be fined for not going to the meeting. There were others in which you were not allowed into the meeting if you did not wear a tall silk hat, and a frock coat, and a bow tie. I am not exaggerating. The rules used to state you had to be 'properly dressed'. To be properly dressed, of course, cost an arm and a leg. When the first dockers' union delegates went to the TUC, there was a famous row. John Burns, that great spokesman of the dock strike who was elected as an MP in 1892, wrote an article in which he pointed out that the skilled workers were not only better turned out, but also all taller, stouter, better built, and smoother than these ragged individuals that now came in representing the dockers. Burns was accused of something close to racism for saying this, but it was the sober truth.

As these people organised themselves all their skills and all their inventiveness found an outlet. They were making and shaping a political process. That process led to the formation of the Labour Party, and it also led to the extension of the franchise. This became unavoidable during the First World War, because millions of voteless men were mown down to save 'their country'.

After conscription came in, it could not even be said they were volunteers. Clearly it was indefensible to be herded into war and slaughter without the right to vote on whether to support the hostilities or not. The call for male suffrage led to the universal franchise in which women were able to vote, and in which general elections could begin to register the actual opinions of the British population. And the first time that that happened was in the period immediately after the First World War. That is the date of British modern democracy, and you can say really that the whole of that process is covered in *The Making of the Labour Movement*. There was, in fact, at the beginning of the story, no political democracy in this country: there was a club of the oligarchs, but at the end of the story rudimentary popular democracy was beginning to assert itself, and the people were beginning to find a way to express themselves.

At the forefront of that popular movement were the so-called unskilled workers, the lesser breeds, the ones with dirty hands, the ones who could not dress in the proper attire, the ones who were outside the pale. That's an extraordinary story!

People should be very proud of these traditions. It is really the uncelebrated story of everything that is good in Britain. The last thing I should say is that in the processes which led to all these developments, there was a very important juncture.

When you began to organise against the indifference and hostility of an enfranchised minority, you had to look which way you could go in order to express the democratic will, and among the people who joined the dockers' union the day after the great dock strike were two branches in Sweden, another branch in Holland. What were they doing? Port workers everywhere had the same interests. Seamen everywhere had the same interests. From the beginning, they saw their interests as involving a linkage, like with like. The workers had no country. They really did not have a country, they could not vote where they lived, they had no power there: but they had a common interest with other workers doing the same jobs that they were doing in another country, in which they, too, could not vote. Furthermore, if they all stood together, they could prevail, because they could impose recognition on all the employers in all the ports around the globe. The dockers during the dock strike would have been starved back to work if it had not been for the raising of tens of thousands of pounds by Australian trade unionists. This gave the impulse to an enormous movement of international support and solidarity.

What we tend not to see is that it also was a choice: were you going to organise nationally? In that case you had to organise a political party, and you had to win the vote. To cap that you then had to win the electorate, and you then had to go through all the political processes. Or were you going to organise internationally? In that case you could create brand new institutions, because there wasn't any international parliament. So you could 'do it yourself' by assembling an overwhelming force, which would mean that people would have to listen to the voices that you represented.

There was a long struggle between these two roads to democracy. It was finally resolved when the governments of Western Europe gave in to popular pressure and conceded the popular vote. To make this happen it took a world war in which millions of people were killed.

Our story has been completely different since then, because in every country, and above all in Britain, once we got the vote it meant that our main way forward was national, because we could organise, we could win elections, we could put people in the government, we could change the policy. Obviously common sense said that you combine collective bargaining and political mobilisation, and on the national plane that was your way forward. Now, of course, we are coming round in a circle, because at the national plane we find we do all these things, and we win an election, and yet still we can't change anything, because all the industrial forces have now become international themselves, and they confront us with the kind of power that our unions never had, but that they were seeking to get, back at the end of the nineteenth century. They confront us with immense power, and we shan't win it back until we unite our forces at least as closely in order to be able to bargain for the people that we represent,

31

whether they live in Sicily or in Denmark or in Birmingham. That's a new agenda, a really powerful agenda, but it's an agenda which I think you get enormous help in meeting if you work through the experiences of our grandfathers and great-grandfathers in the story that we've been trying to tell. There is nothing new under the sun. Actually, this history is as much about tomorrow as it is about yesterday.

First published in 1991

2

Democracy and Workers' Control

This essay was published in 1965 by Fontana Books in Towards Socialism, *a collection edited by Perry Anderson and Robin Blackburn. This was an attempt by the editors of* New Left Review *to come to grips with the challenge of a new Labour Government, and the rise of Harold Wilson as the Leader of the Labour Party.*

Looking at the trade union basis of this Labour Movement, it is clear that democratisation at that time still had a remarkable way to go. In the Transport and General Workers' Union, a period of bureaucratic atrophy under the leadership of Arthur Deakin had come to end, and after a very brief interregnum in which Jock Tiffin was elected General Secretary, his premature death brought Frank Cousins to office, with an important promise of renewal. This was not before time, since the Union's hold over some important parts of its membership was weakening and there had been worrying signs or even threats of breakaways, which raised the fear of disintegration. Frank Cousins established a forceful leadership, which restored the sense of trade union integrity.

But in other unions, oligarchy still ruled, as for example in the powerful Engineers' Union, which was led by Sir William (later Lord) Carron, who showed a fine disregard for the unruly sentiments of a growing part of his membership. His militant shop stewards, for instance, he described as 'werewolves'.

Carron's cavalier use of the block vote, in which he frequently unilaterally overruled the governing National Committee of his Union, to cast the vote of the entire membership of his Union in favour of his personal choices, flatly opposing membership opinion, gave rise to growing discontent among the engineers. Ernie Roberts, a strong voice for workers' control and industrial democracy, was a leading spokesman for the opposition. He occupied the position of Assistant General Secretary, but found himself surrounded by hostile officials who took their cue from the leadership. Nonetheless, a growing sense of abuse took root among the engineers, and found expression in their rank and file newspaper, edited by Roberts, called Engineers' Voice. *This became a key component of the series of Workers' Control conferences which were later to lead to the formation of the Institute for Workers' Control.*

Meantime, the New Left Review was one of several journals and groupings which gave hospitality to the new ideas which found tentative expression in this essay.

The term 'workers' control'- is commonly used to cover two quite distinct concepts. One maintains, in the words of the German socialist Thaiheimer, that 'control over production signifies the management of the industries by the workers', and usually appears in discussion as an attempt to outline an ideal norm of administration for socialised industries In this tradition, one finds that in Britain, throughout the nineteen-thirties, speakers in TUC debates on the popular administration of nationalised industries almost invariably used the term in this sense. But another tradition has evolved a quite different concept which speaks of 'workers' control' in those contexts where militant trade unions have been able to wrest some, or most, of the prerogatives of management from the unilateral disposition of managers.

It is misleading to use the same term to speak of two such different conditions. To do so implies that an unbroken continuity of democratic advance stretches between the imposition of a trade union veto on dismissals and the ultimate overcoming of capitalist property relations. This is a naïve view, because it completely ignores the deforming power of these property relations in the generation both of ideology and of social forces beyond democratic control. In a climate in which all human relationships are founded on cash-values, the most flagrantly anti-social and irresponsible acts of capital appear as 'natural' events, beyond the scope of social control.

What appears to be 'fair' in such a structure is very remote from what would seem so in a society uncluttered by the domination of institutions of property. Even active trade unionists, who will respond most vigorously to changes in their conditions of work when these appear to be unfair, very seldom break through the given standards of our society to form any conception of the incomparably richer and more humane standards which a classless society would create. Within the compass of this ideology, generated by it and constantly reinforcing it, lies the power of the state. This power, far from giving expression to democratic initiative, inhibits and frustrates it. Nowhere in this more clearly to be seen than in the field of industrial relations, in which the state has consistently intervened to contain or transmute pressures for democratic control into harmless experiments permitting the sovereignty of property institutions to survive unimpaired.

But even if these things were not true, and the continuous encroachment of democracy in industry were assured, we should still require at some point in its progress the recognition of a qualitatively different set of problems. It seems incorrect to speak of 'workers' control' where ultimate authority is supposed to rest with the workers, because 'control' is a term which implies a more or less involved apparatus of checks, or even vetoes, by one party on the behaviour of another. The demand for workers' control, thus literally interpreted, becomes a demand, explicit or implicit, for a reversal of roles in a class-divided society. The workers wish to limit the scope of the action of other *persons,* of managers or owners, and not merely, as is often implied, to 'control' inanimate objects such as their machines and raw materials. Inanimate objects appear to be at stake, because reification is at work; what the machines do is not the result of any will of their own, but of the outcome of a tussle of wills between people, whose relationships have been refracted through things and camouflaged in the process. Whether at the level of shop control of hire-and-fire, and agreements on 100 per cent trade union membership, or at the level of detailed union inspection of a firm's account books and workers' veto on investment decisions and the distribution of profits, workers' control in this sense involves a balance of hostile forces, a division of authority between rival contenders.

Once property and its taboos are overcome, this mobile, dual relationship ceases to exist. The new problem becomes one of democratic self-regulation. This is a very different concern from that which faces the Labour Movement this side of the socialist transformation of private property into common wealth. A recognition of this fact is implied in the interesting experiences of – among others – the Yugoslavs and the Algerians. The Algerians invariably speak of the administrative system of their nationalised concerns as '*autogestion*', while the Yugoslavs use the term 'self-management' to describe the government of their socialised sector. Following this usage, it seems sensible for us to speak of 'workers' control' to indicate the aggressive encroachment of trade unions on management powers in a capitalist framework, and of 'workers' self-management' to indicate attempts to administer a socialised economy democratically. While insisting that there is most unlikely to be a simple institutional continuity between the two conditions, it seems quite clear that workers' control can be a most valuable school for self-management, and that the notion of self-management can be an important stimulus to the demand for control. Between the two, however it may be accomplished, lies the political transformation of the social structure.

After resting dormant for two generations, the movement for workers' control in Britain has once again begun to stir, reshape itself, and gather force and insight. Already it has become sufficiently explicit to appear as a demand on union conference agendas, in the utterances of important trade union leaders, and in resolutions approved at the Labour Party Conference and Trade Union Congress in 1963.[1] Numerous articles and papers on it have begun to circulate in the socialist and trade union press,[2] and well-attended seminars of academics and trade unionists have convened to discuss it.[3] The interest which it arouses is not, naturally enough, very easily visible in the popular press, or through the other means of communication which are among the perquisites of capital. But neither do the formal commitments of the big trade unions, or statements by their leading personalities, give an adequate idea of the huge powder-keg of workpeople's daily concern about it which could eventually be set off by the lightest, most sensitive of trigger actions.

The basic change in the economic condition of Britain, like that of Western Europe as a whole, is the near-full employment which underpins not only the successes but also all the major problems of neo-capitalism. The social effects of this change have, until recently, been noted simply in the shape of obtrusive and often misleading marks of affluence. Up to the beginning of this decade, affluence was almost universally equated with working-class apathy, enervation, and depoliticisation. The election result of October 1964 has provided its own commentary on this view of things. There is some evidence that the Labour victory was the result of a major renovation of traditional working-class loyalties, resulting in a large working-class poll. By and large the middle strata stayed shy of the Labour Party[4]. This working-class feeling came as no surprise to more thoughtful analysts. The Cambridge sociologists Goldthorpe and Lockwood, in their paper 'Affluence and the British Class Structure'[5] concluded in 1963 that in so far as the traditional communal solidarity of some sections of the British working class has become attenuated, and 'instrumental collectivism' has come to replace it, this in no way underwrites the conservative cause, although it may from time to time assist it. Quite possibly the more calculating, rationalistic assessment of interests implied in the new outlook may result in a radicalisation of working-class politics. To the extent that workers expect improved living standards to be accompanied by improved status, a strain is thrown on the received social structure. If that structure cannot adapt to allow recognition of new status, then something will give. That something may not be the aspirations of the workers.

Unquestionably, the main battlefront of the real status-war is not the suburb. There, problems of social standing have little direct political significance; they are trivialised into the tensions of competing snobberies. The place where status has teeth is beyond all doubt the factory, the office, the enterprise. Here all the brutalising implications of power, from the petty but often infuriating forms it takes in the workshop to the subtly extended and carefully veiled realities at the summits of industry, work into men's souls. The shape of hierarchy in industry was known and felt all too clearly before the war: but it could not become a political issue in any open way while the disciplinary weight of mass-unemployment existed to grind down any protest. Even the socialist case for nationalisation before the war rested almost entirely on grounds of efficiency, and was angled solely at the abolition of unemployment. A job was a goal in such circumstances. Only when stomachs were filled, and relative security established, could people afford to notice the real indignities of their position. Before the war, not only did the worker in work watch his step and count his blessings (the shop stewards' movement disappeared immediately after the First World War, only to show up again in the late thirties, in an aircraft industry whose war contracts provided islands of guaranteed work amid the general insecurity) but the worker out of work, or on short time, aspired above all to a regular job. Post-war workers have not faced these troubles, in the overwhelming majority of cases. Far from being chastened by short-time working, most workers have consistently averaged several hours of overtime[6] a week since the late forties. True, a series of recessions, each one tending to become more pronounced than the last, have served to remind trade unionists of earlier days; while areas of limbo have continued to exist in the north, and in Northern Ireland, providing a dismal exception to the normal story. Yet the ordinary worker has come to form expectations based on continuing full employment, and these are by no means limited to simple economic appetites. Above all, he has come to experience, day in, day out, the taste of capitalism working as nearly as possible to its ideal performance. This is not a sweet taste. Indeed, soothing though it may be to certain directors, for whom things are at their best imaginable, it is becoming increasingly brackish to large numbers of workers.

Their feelings can even be dimly discerned in a book like Ferdinand Zweig's *The Worker in an Affluent Society.*[7] One of his chapters begins: "'Home and work don't mix." This is a phrase which often circulates among working men. It means that "you should leave home at home and work at work", or, "once you leave work, forget it". As one man said, "when you clock out, clock out your mind"... Work matters are rarely mentioned at home ... Work means tension, and home is for relaxation. Men say "I never mention work at home, otherwise I would never relax"[8]. And, towards the end of the book, he writes 'When I asked "Do you like your job?" a generalisation was put forward such as "No one really likes his job"; or to a question "Do you work only for money; does the job give you something else than money?" the answer might be "We all work for money there is nothing else in the job."'[9]

This is the *quiet* response of workers to the working capitalism they have come to know; it is one of dissociation and it is suitable for interviewers. There is a harder response as well.

Faced with psychological withdrawal, and apprehensive about unnecessarily aggravating aspects of the industrial power structure, some leading industrialists have sought ways of mitigating the feel of subordination which is basic to factory organisation as far as employees are concerned.[10] Thus the practice of clocking in, the anomalies of differentials between increasingly routinised clerical workers and shop-floor operatives, the more blatantly inefficient effects of piece-work – all of these have been quite sternly debated not only in the schools of human relations, but among the more perceptive industrial executives themselves. Yet movement is slow. The inertia of British businessmen is perhaps nowhere more recognisable than in this field, where their own interests might be thought to spell out a certain liberalisation. But perhaps this conservative resistance to change is not entirely stupid, since a thaw might produce a greater flow beneath the ice than could be contained within acceptable channels. One thing is very clear: for all the labours of industrial liberals, things are constantly called by their right names on the shop-floor. It is still extremely common for a new recruit to be told upon engagement, by the brisk, sergeant-majorly figure who signs him on, that 'When you start here, it is to work, not think: we pay our own thinkers, and they don't need your help.' Even where the notion that workers are hands, not brains, has been expunged by managerial fiat from the vocabulary of supervision, its reality remains no less painfully obvious. The proliferation of work study and method study techniques serve not only to increase the rate of return per man employed, but also, and perhaps far more damagingly to the man concerned, to strip away with increasing efficiency the last remaining areas of independent decision and initiative which had hitherto survived in the workshop. That such techniques do not necessarily serve to increase productivity[11] seems to present no noticeable obstacle to their advance: it seems clear that they owe at least as much of their popularity to their disciplinary advantages as to their productive merits. The growth and decline of formal means of communication, including suggestion schemes, has done nothing whatever to ameliorate the fact that in modern industry workers are used as mere means to ends formed independently of their will. At best such devices have exposed workers to the unilateral adoption of *their* ideas by others; they provide no long-term assurance that the application of these ideas may not be to their own detriment. The remorseless division of labour which polarises the factory into a small corps of decision-takers on one side, and an army of subordinates on the other does not simply alienate the labour force. The concentration of decision-taking power, untempered by any effective responsible controls, tends to produce a succession of organisational crises in which expensive blunders are followed by brutal reshuffles, as the left hand of management vainly gropes after even the rudiments of knowledge about the movements of its right hand.

Were data available, there can be little doubt that the present incidence of managerial waste would stagger everyone. As things are, it is seldom documented, and almost never openly discussed. But unless the Nottingham area is completely exceptional, it must run into millions every year. Its human cost is unmeasurable, because mistakes that are tiny in terms of revenue can be cataclysmic in their effects on people. In one enterprise in Nottinghamshire, workers were recently engaged to build an annexe, which was subsequently discovered to be in the way of other developments, and therefore scheduled for demolition. This, so far, is a common enough story. But on this job, the demolition gangs moved in to start work while the decorators were still at their task, making habitable the barely completed building. So, while the painters were busily finishing their work on the fourth wall, the other three were being removed by the heavy squads. Some of the workers concerned claim that they were compelled to wait because demolition had to be suspended until the painters finished and got out of the way. Countless similar stories will be retailed to anyone who talks to groups of workers about the problem of waste.

In the nationalised industries the record is no better: I personally have several times been involved in quite large-scale works which were demolished on completion, and have innumerable experiences of installing expensive machines which did not work, or walking past other expensive machines which had lain idle and forgotten for months on end in very damaging conditions. None of these things would be permitted if workpeople were assured of both an interest in production as a whole, and sufficient powers to uphold it. If this is true where a firm's income is at stake, it is even more true where men's dignity and self-respect are involved. One small example of the kind of tragedy that often happens was recorded in the Nottingham press a year ago. It concerns an engineering plant, in which a man was seriously injured by a jet of steam that had been discharged through a grating as he was walking over it. Inquiries revealed that this discharge was the result of a mistake, Another employee had, more than twenty years previously, been detailed to open a valve at certain fixed times of the day, in order to lower available steam-pressure. Many years ago this operation had been made completely unnecessary, because the plant had been adapted in order to make it safe. But no one had ever informed the worker concerned. Year in, year out, he had continued to perform an un-needed task, which was dangerous to others, until an accident interfered to redress the organisation of his work. The feelings of this man, placed in such a situation, are not difficult to imagine. In fact, his workmates reported that he was utterly demoralised by the discovery that he had for years been paid to perform a completely useless and damaging operation. Such instances could be extended indefinitely, but the point should already be clear: the deprivation of responsibility which workers suffer in this sort of situation does not merely damage them personally, as individuals; it is also socially destructive, and constantly undermines the development of productive powers. However vigorously employers seek out means to overcome these difficulties, they are fighting a losing battle. Whilst the product itself remains beyond the control of the workpeople who produce it, their self-protection impels them not merely to suffer such absurd failures of 'organisation', but even to conspire to prevent their alleviation. If you are alienated from the product of your work, such forms of ca'canny as are involved in protecting management from attaining accurate self-knowledge, and sometimes more radical forms of resistance as well, are by no means stupid. You are aware that augmented productivity may turn out to be a weapon for use against you, rather than a straightforward development and extension of your powers. On the national scale, crusades for productivity were summed up in the early months of 1968 by special postage stamps exalting additional effort, while the unemployment figures were mounting week by week.

The main device which has been employed to sidetrack the

frustrations which the authoritarian control of industry induces in its workpeople, and the recurring problems of production which stem from the necessarily abortive attempt to restrict or abolish the initiative of workers, is that of joint consultation. Born in the First World War, an uncertain changeling, it did not survive very long. Between 1918 and 1939 the dole queues provided most employers with all the consultation they felt they needed. But the Second World War brought about a strange reincarnation. Bevin's elevation to the Ministry of Labour coincided with a bizarre turn of fortune, in which the most militant goading force in the unions, the Communist Party, was soon to come out of opposition and play a major role in the crusade for war-production. Effective pioneer of the reborn shop-stewards movement, the Communist Party found itself also pioneering at the rebirth of joint consultation. It demanded the setting up of joint production committees and activated their members. Huge conferences of stewards were held in the glare of enthusiastic press publicity to consider ways of expanding production. All of this had the effect of creating a certain ambivalence among shop-stewards, which did not wear off with the war effort. But the rationality of joint consultation was not ambivalent. The new situation of the early forties required new practices by management, if it was to continue managing for long. Seldom has the argument for these been presented with more disarming frankness than by G. S. Walpole in *Management and Men,* published as a guide to joint consultation in 1944:

> What joint consultation does for industry is threefold in character. It provides the higher management with an additional source of information, warning, and advice – particularly valuable because it covers a field in which conventional channels of information and advice are too often biased or ineffective. It also provides the means for transmitting to employees information and explanation without which their attitude towards their work or their management is liable to be prejudiced. Thirdly, on the psychological side *it canalises the legitimate aspiration of labour to have a voice in the industry to which it contributes so much.*[12] (My italics.)

This canalisation was furthered and consolidated after the election of the post-war Labour Government by the simple device of writing joint consultation procedures into the nationalisation acts governing those industries which Labour took into public ownership. (At the same time, a few eminent trade union leaders found themselves on the boards of these new corporations – in this way ended all the declamatory 'workers' control' talk of the TUC during the thirties.) The net effect of such consultation, whether in public or private sectors, will surprise very few people. For private industry, it has recently been summed up by D. Llewellyn Davies, in a study entitled *Formal Consultation in Practice*. His view is: 'The general impression gained is that the majority of firms do not fully believe in and practise formal consultation and all that it implies, but use it rather as a forum for company pronouncements and the airing of employee irritants.'[13] Even when the employers *do* 'believe in' consultation, of course, all that this can ever mean is that they may seek employees' opinions before they tell them what to do. Such procedures may provide a certain soothing balm during those honeymoons in which competition leaves management free of the need to make sharp turns in policy, with all the consequent upheavals in working conditions which these so frequently involve. But overall, there is no doubt whatever that in recent years they have become increasingly irrelevant.

As evidence of this, we may consider a number of facts. The growth rate of shop-steward representation in the Amalgamated Engineering Union doubled in the period 1957-61, as compared with the period 1947-56.[14] Anthony Topham, in a valuable study published by *New Left Review*,[15] points out:

> 'Associated with this very rapid rate of expansion of numbers of stewards, has been a decline of one-third in formal Joint Consultation Committees, and a corresponding rise in 'domestic' (i.e. plant-level) bargaining. Related to this again, the number of work stoppages has increased in federated establishments [in the Engineering Industry – KC] by 23 per cent and the number of working days lost as a result rose by 82 per cent.'

Direct workshop representation is, in other words, replacing 'the concessionary management device of joint consultation'. In this atmosphere the 'legitimate aspirations' of workpeople to have a say in the control and direction of the enterprises in which they work are less and less capable of being 'canalised', and more and more likely to erupt into their own consciously formulated demands. Until now these demands have tended to remain close to the present

43

experiences of workers, and, as a result, to take on a partial, regional or local significance This tendency has been reinforced by the whole post-war tradition of the shop-stewards' movement, which began its evolution towards the present state of affairs during the Attlee Government's 'wage-freeze', which in Britain was paradoxically responsible for the initial growth of the phenomenon of wage-drift[16] which has recently triggered off such a load of complaints from the National Incomes Commission. As local managements found the need to bid up wages in competition for scarce labour, and shop-stewards discovered both the need to fend for themselves and the possibility of doing it rather well, decentralisation of wage-bargaining set in with a vengeance. Socialist militants have frequently registered the results of this with some pleasure, because it tends to feed the image of an activist rank and file and a lethargic bureaucracy dominating the central apparatus of the unions. This image is by no means without its reference point in reality, but it is often very over-simplified. The price of this decentralisation was high, both in terms of apathy (if local strikes are not 'a private solution to public problems', then at least they are often a less-than-public solution of them), and in terms of fragmentation and loss of political consciousness. It is strange that more attention has not been paid to this phenomenon in relation to the Labour Party's crisis during the fifties – it is no coincidence that Labour's revival came after a number of fierce attacks on the unions by the Conservative administration of 1959-64.

Be that as it may, Topham documents a remarkable change in the character of the shop-stewards. He quotes the findings of Professor Turner[17] on the causes of strikes, as given by strikers themselves: between 1940 and 1960, if one excludes strikes in the mining industry, which is still a separate universe in these matters, the proportion of strikes about wage matters *'other than* demands for increases', or about 'working arrangements, rules and discipline', rose from one-third to three-quarters of the total. This gives us a measure, not simply of the extent of the 'drift', but also of the changing mood of the workers. There is additional evidence on this score. In 1960 the TUC General Council published their report on 'Disputes and Workshop Representation'[18] which analysed the results of four separate questionnaires, covering the cost of dispute pay to affiliated unions between 1956 and 1959, details of both official and unofficial strikes in 1958 and 1959, and details of stoppages in which one union found its members unable to work because members of other unions were on strike. One hundred and forty seven Unions representing seven and a half million workers replied, and this response proved completely unambiguous: only 32 per cent of strikes during that period had been directly about money and these included cases in which workers had been resisting attempts by employers to reduce wages; 29 per cent were about dismissals, 20 per cent were caused by disciplinary dismissals of stewards or other members, and 9 per cent concerned redundancies. The remainder were about recognition, non-unionism, breach of agreements, changes in work systems, demarcation and dilution, bad working conditions or complaints about supervisors. When the unions concerned were able to differentiate between 'underlying causes' as opposed to stated causes, this had the effect of still further reducing the proportion of disputes over wages. The power of shop-stewards was originally fostered and extended by the growth of local negotiations about wages. The strike-record makes it clear that their power is now firmly rooted, and able to burgeon into very much wider fields.

If one accepts that strikes are still relatively uncommon occurrences in British industry, and moves on to examine the normal working of shop-stewards in less turbulent conditions, this story is sharply confirmed. According to Clegg, Killick and Adams, in their survey *Trade Union Officers*,[19] which contains a comprehensive study of the role of stewards in the working of the unions, the average steward spends six hours a week of his working time and five of his own on a whole range of trade union duties. By far the most important of these concern negotiations with foremen and managers. Following these in importance, as a proportion of stewards' time, comes the item 'consultation with constituents and discussions with other stewards'. Together these took up 69 per cent of the time spent on union business by stewards covered in the survey.[20] When the same stewards were asked to define the priority of their trade union aims,[21] 23 per cent of them thought that first was 'better wages and conditions'. But 21 per cent thought that the main thing was '100 per cent organisation', 14 per cent that it was 'creating unity between workers', and 10 per cent that it was 'fullest use by the rank and file of the democratic procedures of the union'. With 5 per cent who put 'creating political consciousness' first, this amounts to 50 per cent who saw their main trade union aims as turning around the development and consolidation of workpeople's *power.* Of course, this power will lever pence out of the employers: but it also poses them with deeper problems, to which cash offers no immediate solution. Even when one looks at the 19 per cent who put first the priority 'effective consultation with the management', one may suspect that this does not always mean quite what the official propagandists of consultation expect.

The sum of these developments has been calculated and expressed by a whole number of close observers of the industrial landscape, many of whom are very far from being disaffected radicals. Speaking of 'something like a revolution in our industrial relations', Arthur Marsh notes that full employment has extended the trade union expectations of craftsmen to all the workers, who, since the war, have 'been able to rely more on the fact that employers have been competing for labour of all kinds, that they have been reluctant to lose workers, and unable and unwilling to back their authority by large-scale or selective dismissals. *Work group sanctions against management have gradually become effective, and 'management by consent' generally necessary.'*[22] To this picture, Alan Flanders adds:

> 'The steward's formal role under our traditional system of collective bargaining was largely that of watchdog and policeman. Earnings drift has rendered that view of their role totally unrealistic. Today they are negotiators in their own right, *rule makers as well as rule enforcers.'*[23]

It would be wrong to find in these signs an omen of immediately impending upheaval. Shop-stewards are – contrary to the Press image of them – responsible men. Their average age is in the forties. They have family responsibilities which weigh as heavily on them as on their workmates. The political implications of their situation do not confront them in clear, lucid prescriptions, but are refracted through a fog of local prejudices, overlapping and at times conflicting group interests, irrational organisational boundaries. At the head of their unions often stand, not the kind of men who can see over all the territory and pierce its obscurities with the insight drawn from a live movement of many thousands of people, but anxious, timid and purblind intriguers, who try to chart their paths through an alien countryside (which they imagine they know well) by landmarks which have long since ceased to exist (and which they recreate in their imagination, hazier each time, day by day). Beyond these structural deformities in the vision of the Labour Movement, lies the mystery of capitalist property relations itself.

But today the problems which capital itself has created are fiercely sharpening the outlines, and settling the fog. Neo-capitalism is forced to 'plan', to rationalise itself, and above all to constrain and discipline its labour force; in doing so, it precipitates new problems and objectives for the unions. The pace at which this has occurred has noticeably increased in the past few years. Indeed, the election of a Labour government is only one early result of its gathering force, and by no means the ultimate one. Having created the wage-drift, and reactivated the trade unions on a local, fragmented basis, neo-capitalism is now in the process of recentralising them, and giving them new, more integrated and probing policies. But just as the rise of stewards' power was not the result of an act of will by the employers, even though many of them individually fed it and contributed to it, so this new co-ordination is not likely to fall into the set patterns which would enable the established powers to approve it. To be sure, there are now many strange new advocates of industrial unions, as the business press begins to evaluate the effects of 'anarchy' in the Unions on the new planning machinery which is being established. But the unions have not up to now proved amenable to such schemes: if they are to regroup, and streamline their organisations, then very many of their members will insist that this must be under their own initiative, in pursuit of their own objects. Paradoxically, this process has been assisted by the very attacks which have been launched to inhibit trade union powers. The effect of pay pauses, National Incomes Commissions, rationalisation schemes of the Beeching variety, and even the notorious *Rookes versus Barnard* judgement which placed the right to strike itself in jeopardy, has been to stimulate political consciousness and to turn trade union activists away from narrow sectionalism.

Clearly the pursuit of political answers to some of the most urgent problems faced by shop-stewards does not in the least imply any retreat from gains won locally. At the local level, the Unions will remain combative, jealous of their powers, and anxious to develop their strength. New political tasks do not in the least imply that one should let go of control of hire and fire, or give away rest breaks, or abandon any of the powers which have been wrested away from the formerly unchallenged disposition of management. On the other hand, the defence of such gains itself comes to insist that a larger view of the world be taken, and that effective nation-wide resistance be offered to the concerted probes which have recently been undertaken to test whether any of the Unions' gains can be recouped from them. The most serious of these probes is beyond any doubt the sustained pressure for an incomes policy, which has simultaneously taken shape in almost every country in Europe in the last few years, and which threatens *all* the major union advances in a very direct manner.[24]

The campaign for an incomes policy poses on a new plane the very old problem of how capital can co-exist with a powerful trade union movement. Beneath all the trimmings of welfare in which neo-capitalism is bedecked, this basic conflict has in no way been resolved. Now, however, neo-capitalism faces many closed doors which were at one time open to its forerunners. Above all, the pre-war disciplinary force of sustained unemployment, running into millions, is not an option today. Meanwhile, international competition demands that margins be considered ever more tightly, and basic costs be budgeted over longer periods within narrower limits of fluctuation. Hence the overriding concern about inflation, and the constant pre-occupation with the 'stabilisation' of wage-costs. Wages must be brought under control if the cutting edge of capital is not to be dulled to a degree intolerable to its masters.

Those spokesmen of the labour movement who are closest to the acceptance of neo-capitalism pure and simple have already drawn an appropriate moral from this. They see the role of the Labour government as being that of rationaliser-extraordinary to a system which is short-winded, queazy and directionless. To liberate the power of efficient and well-directed greed, they will happily treat with the unions, offering to exchange such meagre cash-benefits as they can afford against a surrender of power. So, well-known Fabians write of a controlled war against wage-drift, which of course involves quite simply an offensive against the powers of shop-stewards:[25] they speak of the 'relegation of collective bargaining machinery to a secondary place in the structure':[26] and they discuss the price which Unions may or may not demand as compensation for loss of powers in this realm.[27] In all this can be discerned a pattern of authoritarian paternalism, which assumes a standard of 'fairness' in income distribution which has only to be announced, and then applied by civil servants, to produce universal harmony and rocketing economic advance. In fact, no such standard is possible: while the overwhelming majority of goods are distributed on the market, and not by means of welfare services, 'fairness' will always be determined in the course of argument and the interplay of rival interests, unless totalitarian edicts are to prescribe its limits. More: far from representing a drag on productivity, this argument is generally a stimulus to it. Certainly, under capitalism, union demands represent a continual goad to technological advance, indeed, they often pose the most serious questions of organisation that are ever faced by an increasingly lethargic economic directorate. This point was made, in a heavy-handed way, by Charles Babbage as long ago as 1832, and it has lost none of its force with the concentration of industrial power and the growth of bureaucratic forms of administration. Paternalist Fabianism is in great danger when it plays with these types of policy. Its advocates seldom show any awareness of the extent to which all the freedoms that they empirically support are underpinned by the existence of an independent trade union movement. The statification of Union powers clearly demands fierce inroads in the freedom of movement of unions, above all at local level. In the last analysis, unions do not exist anywhere else than at local level. If apathy and demoralisation set in at the root, the leading trade union 'planners', who flit from office to office in Whitehall in order to discuss guesses about production levels and fiats about wages, will become increasingly empty poseurs.[28] Without active and politically alive shop-stewards behind them, they can be discarded by any government commission which tires of them. As for the Labour Party, without enthusiasm in the factories it is a shroud for unattained dreams.

A heavy responsibility rests, then, on trade union activists under a Labour government. Confronted with crisis on a dozen fronts at once, the Labour government will insistently press for agreement on an incomes policy. This places the unions between two perils. If they agree, their vital powers are at stake. If they refuse, they must fear the fall of the government, which cannot be seen as an advantage to the workers. What, then, is to be done?

It is here that the traditional demand for workers' control takes on a new meaning, gathering a hard relevance that can turn it from a concern of a few militants into the central strategic demand of the day. The unions can hardly refuse to negotiate with their own government on incomes policy. But they can set their own price for starting talks, provided it is reasonable. And the elementary price for beginning a discussion on incomes policy is hard information about what incomes *are*.

If such data are secured by the unions, it may still not result in an acceptable policy on incomes: and they may be compelled to stand their ground on other issues. But at least they will know the score, talks will be conducted on an almost equal footing (almost, because workers' inspection of the accounts only adds to the *risk* involved in distorting them, and will in any case vary in efficiency and rigour) and judgments will therefore lack the perilous, gambling uncertainty with which they will otherwise undoubtedly be fraught.

This approach would remove some of the shibboleths engendered by the dominance of private property over men's minds. The present pattern of rewards, and the absurd tolerance of the private appropriation of the results of public effort, will come to seem far less 'natural'. When they see precisely how far 'self-financing' has become the norm in private industry, workers will begin to wonder why the results of their effort cannot be invested in their own name rather than to the credit of some *rentier*. Clause Four of the Labour Party's constitution will cease to be an inspirational icon. From an intensification of the campaign for workers' control, we shall prepare for the leap towards new political and social forms, to self-management.

The transition to socialism in Britain is not necessarily a matter of decades. The weight of the problems of capitalism is so heavy and their effect has so disoriented the political guides and leaders of the system, that it seems clear that it is only the inertia and lack of insight of the Labour Movement that allows the whole system to continue. To develop a strategy of advance is the crucial task of the Left today: but this cannot be done if we are not prepared to discuss socialism itself. The goal will cast its own shape on the path we beat towards it.

To say that duality of power ceases to exist once industry is socialised would be a truism, were the word 'socialised' to refer not merely to the juridical ownership of plant, but also to the product. If socialist, or welfare, forms of distribution were general, many present conflicts would be inconceivable. These conflicts arise essentially between opposed interests, which generate opposed ideals, appealing to property and democracy respectively. Although the antithetical natures of private property and democracy are often obscured, deliberately, by ideologists who offer verbal resolutions of the real contradiction, and as a reflex response by people who are thinking within a climate in which it appears as 'natural', none the less it is constantly reasserted in the struggles which take place every day in almost every enterprise. On workpeople's side, the development of democratic ideas under capitalism is inseparable from the development of solidarity. Yet this solidarity is not to be interpreted, as it has been on many occasions, as a founding charter for monolithic discipline in *socialist* factories. The problem of self-management begins with a recognition that each worker has a complex of interests, often divergent ones, involving him as consumer, as producer and as citizen. These must persist as long as the division of labour itself compels men to adopt fixed roles during formative parts of their lives. Such interests will align him with some other men into shifting groups and lobbies, and oppose him to some other men at every major turn of the decision-making process. Either these interests will achieve open and satisfying expression, or they will be muffled, frustrated, and thwarted, thus producing an inhibiting apathy which will drive them further and further underground, sterilising the creative force which they represent.

Yet those who have witnessed this process at work in countries in which the democratic process has been paralysed over long periods, frequently identify it with the dehumanisation of labour under capitalist relations of production, and then telescope all problems of dehumanisation together, locating them all in the problem of the popular administration of industry. This is mistaken. The traditional socialist answer to the search for the source of the dehumanisation of labour under capitalism involves an integrated critique of the force of the market and the division of labour which it produces: these phenomena express themselves in forms of property. Unless the constrictions of private property can be overcome, we cannot begin to get to grips with the problem of overcoming the tyranny of the market, and with it the division of labour itself. This means that for a socialist the problem of the market can never be a secondary one. Our strategy can never be limited to moves designed to ameliorate the labour process (desirable in themselves though these may be), because our problem is that of overcoming the compulsion to labour itself, and abolishing with it the whole preformed and viciously mutilating division of labour which aligns men into classes and divides classes into castes, stamping rank on the faces of people and dissolving their common humanity. How far can labour be humanised by democratising industry? The answer is complex: but some things about it are very simple indeed. If we speak of humanising labour,[28] we are speaking of developing the labourer's freedom. This freedom is a capacity for self-realisation, or it is nothing. But we are members of one another. Ourselves are not preformed atoms, but learnt from the people around us in reciprocal human action. For this reason, the division of labour, having opened doors to freedom, becomes a cruel barrier to it. A democratically-run sandfoundry is a far better place than one run by order: but in a world where some men ride round the moon or sing in *Fidelio* a foundryman is not a *free* man. To secure an explosion in the amount of free time, in which men can travel, work, design or speculate by turns as their wish takes them, we must liberate a technological and productive explosion which can underpin it. Of course, this requires a planned, co-ordinated effort. But precisely here, in the pursuit of the goal of freedom, we find the commonest alibi for ignoring what remains a vital question, that of self-management.

For self-management is essentially a problem of democratic planning. It would be foolish to assume that this is solved, even at the blueprint stage. Whilst we can learn something important from experiments which have already been made, we have most of the work to do ourselves. Even in Yugoslavia, the problem is so far from being solved that it is not impossible that we may yet regard that country as an object-lesson in pit-falls, rather than the brave pilot which it looked like being in the beginning. The Yugoslav assumption that the encroachment of bureaucracy can only be combated by decentralisation and increased sensitivity to the demands of the market, tends to reduce the question of democratic control to one of an increasingly meaningless local autonomy, and gradually replaces a central, conscious, willed network of decisions by impalpable and unseen economic pressures. The market calls out for power to repair the damage done by the market, and a complex of incentives invades even hospitals and schools in a vain attempt to check bureaucracy by increasing differentials. All this feeds the fragmentation of workpeople, and multiplies their apathy. This makes it increasingly difficult to evolve corrective policies. One hopes this pessimistic picture will be falsified. But the Yugoslav experience reinforces the view that the key to the problem of democratic planning involves the discovery of means by which we can institutionalise, and thereby legitimise, conflicts about the priorities of the master plan itself. Such conflicts are bound to be serious even in the most advanced countries, where they are extremely unlikely to be resolved in appeals to charismatic forces and individuals 'above the battle'.

To see these difficulties is not to solve them. The solutions will not be easy, and are unlikely to be reached by a process of speculation. Men will hammer out their institutions on the problems that they face with the forces that they have. It is a very practical process, and it gets into books after it has happened. But we have half a century of warnings about some of the problems of the transition we will soon be entering, and we would be fools to ignore them.

But we can clear the way for action. In less than a generation we *can* see, if we wish it, the beginnings of a new style of men, who will have miles to grow and universes to subdue, but who will never have taken an order, or been afraid of other men, or done an action without knowing why.

First published in 1965

Footnotes

1. See *Report of the Labour Party Conference*, 1963, pp. 189-90 *Trades Union Congress Report*, 1963, pp. 276, 460 and *Trades Union Congress Report*, 1964, pp. 321, 446, 489. The TUC discussions involve 'workers' participation in the nationalised industries.' This is an ambiguous term, which can mean anything from Joint Consultation (as it does, obviously, to many members of the General Council) up to full workers' management of nationalised enterprises.

2. The most radical and coherent appeal yet has come from Ernie Roberts, Assistant General Secretary of the AEU. In the broadsheet issued with the Autumn 1964 issue of *Voice of the Unions*, he puts forward a comprehensive plan for the administration of the steel industry after nationalisation. This would have the effect of bringing 'participation' up to the point of workers' management: 'Each shop would have its own elected Shop Committee which would send delegates to a central Works Council. The Shop Committee would also elect its supervision, and the Works Councils would appoint higher management. The Board of the enterprise would have representatives from the State agency, charged with implementing the plan, and representatives from the Works Councils, responsible for details of production.' Unions would negotiate with this Board about the distribution of the surplus and conditions of work, just as they would today. Such a scheme would have the dual effect of popularising nationalisation, which is generally construed as a bureaucratic monster, and, at the same time, ensuring that the nationalised industry did not simply subserve the private sector, but made its own pace. *Voice of the Unions* has announced a campaign in the steel producing areas around this platform: its outcome could be extremely important for the advance of British socialism.

3. One, at Nottingham, attacted 140 participants drawn from most unions and a number of universities. Reports of it have appeared in *Tribune* (May, 1964), *New Left Review*, No. 25, pp. 13-16, *Anarchy*, No. 40, June, 1964, and *The Week*, vol. II, No. 4, July, 1964. *Hull Left*, published by Labour Students at Hull University, reproduced a number of papers which had been submitted for the consideration of the seminar.

4. See the study on the election in *The Observer*, 18 October, 1964.

5. J. H. Goldthorpe and D. Lockwood, 'Affluence and the British Class Structure.' *The Sociological Review*, vol. XI, No. 2, July, 1963, pp. 133-64.

6. Many of which have been unnecessary, according to H. A. Clegg, 'Implications of the Shorter Working Week for Management', *British Institute of Management* Pamphlet, 1962.

7. 1961.

8. Ibid, p. 84.

9. Ibid, p.199

10. See, for example, W. Brown's well-known *Piecework Abandoned*.

11. This has been lucidly demonstrated by Georges Friedmann in his masterly *Industrial Society*, 1955, and in *The Anatomy of Work*, 1961.
12. G. S. Walpole, *Management and Men*, 1944, p. 43.
13. Industrial Welfare Society, 1962.
14. Cf. A. T. Marsh and E. E. Coker, 'Shop Steward Organisation in Engineering', *British Journal of Industrial Relations*, vol. I, No. 2.
15. Shop Stewards and Workers' Control', *New Left Review*, No. 25, May-June, 1964, p5.
16. See above
17. H. A. Turner, *The Trend of Strikes*, 1963, p 8, cited Topham, op. cit., p.6.
18. TUC *Report*, pp. 125-6.
19. 1961.
20. Clegg, Killick and Adams, pp. 149-80.
21. Ibid, p. 262.
22. Arthur Marsh, *Managers and Shop Stewards*, Institute of Personnel Management, l963,p.17.
23. In a paper on 'The Importance of Shop Stewards'.
24. Some useful documentation on this appears in *International Socialist Journal*, No. 3, June 1964. The issue includes a general analysis by Vittorio Foa, Deputy Secretary of the Italian C.G.I.L., and reports on the state of play in England, France, Italy and Federal Germany.
25. Cf. W. E. J. McCarthy, 'The Price of Wage Restraint'. *New Society*, 5 March 1964.
26. Cf. Stewart and Winsbury. 'An Incomes Policy for Labour', *Fabian Tract*, 1963.
27. McCarthy, op. cit. Others, including, rather terrifyingly, Ray Gunter, who is now Minister of Labour, have allowed themselves to discuss this matter in more brutal terms. A heated controversy on Gunter's views broke out in the AEU Journal in mid-1964.
28. If we do, strictly speaking we are erring. The humanisation of *work* involves the *abolition* of labour, as Marx was concerned to point out again and again.

3

Wage Slaves

The New Left Review *continued its advocacy in a book directed at trade unionists, published in 1967 by Penguin Books, under the title* The Incompatibles. *This was edited by Robin Blackburn and Alexander Cockburn. It included this paper, written shortly before the formation of the IWC.*

Meantime, the opposition within the Engineers' Union was gathering strength, and culminated in the election of a new President for the Union, Hugh Scanlon.

Hugh Scanlon represented something very different from the autocratic Bill Carron, and his elevation to the Presidency was accompanied by a strong renewal throughout the Union, which retained powerful democratic roots, and needed but the slightest encouragement to reassert itself. This is what made the formation of the Institute for Workers' Control as a formal organisation, with an elected Council, and a regular programme of conferences and seminars, pretty much inevitable. The argument had begun to grow beyond ad hocery, and to reach out across many industries and services. Later, in 1969, the retirement of Frank Cousins as General Secretary of the Transport and General Workers' Union saw the election of Jack Jones, a passionate advocate of industrial democracy, as his successor. This was to become the age of the 'terrible twins', Jones and Scanlon.

More than thirty years ago, a sensitive adult educationalist published a series of extracts from the writings of his students about their attitudes to their work. These students had all been active trade unionists, men of above average resourcefulness and intelligence. Their accounts of the feel of factory life were uniformly forbidding.

A minder in a cotton spinning mill described his work:

> The mule is fed by boys and the process-work of turning the partly prepared cotton sieves into yarn is controlled by the spinner who is termed the minder. The machine dominates my work. I have to follow every movement of the mule, and as the speed increases so must I. If I leave the machine the broken threads accumulate and the mule must be stopped whilst the broken ends are pierced.[1]

A colliery screen-hand wrote, in a distinctly familiar vein:

> 'Coal comes past me on an endless belt, and it is my duty to separate any dirt there may be from the coal. The belt sets the pace at which I must work. I have no feeling of power when working at the machine: on the contrary, I feel dwarfed, and I feel that the machine, instead of serving man, has become his master.'[2]

Another miner described his attempts to keep pace with underground machinery:

> 'One machine was vomiting more than I could clean up, the other had a larger mouth than I could fill. The outcome was a constant worry: I was working always at the top speed without any sense of rhythm. I often wished that all machines and the men who made them were in hell burning.'[3]

These workers all went up to Ruskin College in the early 1930s. One who completed the course there some time earlier was the engineer, R. M. Fox, whose description of his work, published in 1928, is still vivid:

> 'The invariable comment when the leaving-off hooter sounds is, "there's the one I've been waiting for all day!" And in the morning when the starting signal is given, they mutter "Roll on the second one!" They look forward every day to the end of so many hours of life. Such an attitude towards work cannot embody the final wisdom of the ages.'[4]

This picture is one which I understand from the inside in a rather particular way: long before I ever meditated on it, I had become accustomed to the greeting which all Nottinghamshire miners exchange every morning: 'How are you?' – 'I'll be all right on Friday!' After nine years of such a customary greeting, I went to university. For several weeks I astonished students who asked me how I was by informing them that I would be all right on Friday. It was with a real sense of realisation that it dawned on me one day that Friday was no different from any other day in my new calendar, where freedom ran all through the week. This experience helps to persuade me that things are not so different today, and that the industrial regime of the 1960s is much less of an advance upon its forerunners than most public relations men are prepared to admit.

In 1965, another worker, from a tobacco factory, on his way up to Ruskin, wrote an article for *New Left Review* just before he moved:

'...The other day I overheard two old employees who had been in the factory to receive their pensions. They greeted each other as I passed. "How's it going, Bert?" said the first, "Lovely, Bill" the other, recently retired, replied. "Anything's better than that bloody hole." This may seem a paradoxical reference to a place where someone has spent forty years of his life...

It is probably wrong to expect factories to be other than they are. After all, they are built to house machines, not men. Inside a factory it soon becomes obvious that steel brought to life by electricity takes precedence over flesh and blood. The onus is on the machines to such an extent that they appear to assume the human attributes of those who work them. Machines have become as much like people as people have become like machines. They pulsate with life, while man becomes the robot. There is a premonition of man losing control, an awareness of doom. The machines seem to squat restless in their oily beds awaiting the coming of some mechanical messiah...

Sometimes I have an urge to open the nearest door and walk and walk and walk. I feel a need to get away from this atmosphere of here and now, where all that matters is the present, good or bad, and one must make the best of it. Nobody desires change. Everybody is looking into an endless flat future and thinking they could be worse off.'[5]

Of course, all this is impressionistic evidence. It is also tiresomely familiar. Satanic mills have been part of our landscape since the industrial revolution itself, and the romantic protest against them, however one-sided and utopian it has sometimes been, has provided a fearsome documentation. The alienation of this Nottingham tobacco worker was pinpointed by Herman Melville over a century ago, with his piercing if now depreciated metaphor of the cogs:

'Machinery, the vaunted slave of humanity, here stood menially served by human beings, who served mutely and cringingly, as the slave serves the sultan. The girls did not so much seem accessory wheels to the general machinery as mere cogs to the wheels.'[6]

The condition has also been thoroughly and blisteringly documented in the first volume of Marx's *Capital*. More recently it has been analysed and broken into a whole range of potentially accessible problems by Friedmann, while it has given rise to fierce complaint by the founder of cybernetics, who devoted a whole book to:

'a protest against the inhuman use of human beings'.[7]

It is hardly curious that clever and perceptive workers continue to write this sort of description of their lives, registering their humanity in their protest against the 'inhuman use' which is made of them. From time to time their complaints are heard by investigating sociologists; the problem of alienation, often somewhat hazily apprehended, is becoming increasingly frequently discussed by academics. What is strange is that there also exists a general and dominant mythology which hinges on the official belief that, with 'affluence' and modern man-management, this kind of difficulty is under control, and that factories have been transmuted into a new style of living. These complaints, for all their undeniable onesidedness, indicate very plainly that in spite of half a century of declarations that Labour 'has ceased to be a commodity', the moral status of workers today is in no fundamental sense different from what it was a hundred years ago, while *Das Kapital* was still being read in galley-proof. Naturally, these harrowing commentaries by escapees from the mesh of factory life do not accurately represent the whole of it: it would be fair to say that even in the most estranged environment workers will discover some way of being involved in their work, some small sense of achievement, however attenuated, covert and harassed. What these repeated cries of pain indicate is that the *normal* condition in industry is one of semi-captivity: that inside the prison an occasional bird may sing is not denied.

In any case, individual descriptions of the feel of work are by no means the only evidence about the situation of labour in modern Britain. Lord Robens recently complained that voluntary absenteeism in the mining industry had reached 5.77 per cent of the industry's available manpower, equivalent to a permanent labour force of 27,000 men or an annual £46 million of output. And, in a controversial statement, the Chairman of the National Coal Board also queried the stringency of the criteria used by local practitioners for certifying sickness, on the grounds that involuntary absence has reached new heights. (If there is a heaven to which miners sometimes gain admission, undoubtedly it will include a little window on to purgatory, in which will be labouring, with exemplary fortitude and minute punctuality, all the unlamented legions of Coal Board bureaucrats, productivity-hounds and Labour politicians who ever incited other men to still further intensify a dreary toil which they would not, on earth, even dream of taking, however lightly, and however temporarily, on themselves.)[8] But the collieries are not the only enterprises from which work-people temporarily absent themselves.

Over industry as a whole, sickness absenteeism has been steadily increasing during the past ten years. More than 300 million days a year are now being lost by employed men and women. Particularly important is the increase in psychoneuroses and psychoses. This, for male workers, rose from 13.2 million days of certified incapacity in the year 1953-4, to a provisional estimate of 17.66 million days in 1963-4. The rise in accident rates was even greater, from 12.66 million cases to 18.8 million during the same period. Other, physical, sicknesses have also tended to take a heavier toll in recent years. Dr. Beric Wright, commenting on these facts, points out that:

'all over the world, absentee rates are going up more or less parallel with the growth of social security benefits and hospital services. This overall increase cannot be entirely due to previously untreated disease. We ought as a nation to be fitter than we ever have been, but we are spending more and more time away from work.'[9]

Dr. Wright goes on to advance a diagnosis which is entirely relevant to our argument:

'The problem... is not one of disease, but of lack of job satisfaction and motivation... This becomes clear from the study of the typical businessman. It might be assumed that he can afford to be ill and take long holidays. But the survey carried out by the Institute's (of Directors) Medical Centre showed that directors average between two and three weeks' holiday a year. Some take a month, but overall they do no better than their staff. And they certainly work longer hours. The Medical Centre now has three sets of figures about sickness absence... these show that, including *all* long and short-term sickness, the average director loses only between four and five days a year. Over 60 per cent of directors go for years without losing any time at all. Their sickness rate is about a third that of the rest of the working population.'[10]

Something should be allowed for the fact that directors are their own masters, and can moderate the burdens they lay on themselves when they feel out of sorts, which their employees cannot do. We can allow a little more for the fact that there may be grounds for including under the heading 'work' for directors such burdens as business lunches, sundry rounds of golf, and various other chores which other people might regard as play. On top of this there is the far more telling fact that directors usually vet and submit their own reports on their own activities, a boon not granted to lesser men, whose activities are reported on by others, often without their being given access to the results, and sometimes without their even knowing that reports are being made. Even so, Dr. Wright's argument is not so far-fetched as many workers might think it. 'The more responsible a job, the more strongly motivated its holder, and the more persistent his work', runs its thread. The story is plausible. True, Dr. Wright goes on to attempt to square the circle, by insisting that 'Governments must govern, managements must manage, and everyone needs to work'. The obvious cure for endemic malingering, if the doctor is right about the example of the directors, would be to distribute their mana of responsibility far and wide throughout the populace, in the hope that strong motivation and the virtues of persistence would be distributed with it. Instead, Dr. Wright thinks it necessary to concentrate power, and presumably with it civic and industrial virtue. Yet in spite of this foible, the rest of the diagnosis makes sense. What is remarkable is not that things are as he says they are, but that anyone should expect them to be otherwise. Rational employees might be expected, on working out the balance of advantage, to become disciples of the Good Toiler Schweik, inveterate and skilful malingerers to the last man. The wonder is not that some do, but that most don't. If responsibility carries with it commitment, helotry produces withdrawal: and when Dr. Wright appeals for the sharpening of managerial authority, the stiffening of the division of function, he is in fact appealing for an intensification of the very problem he is trying to solve.

Sickness is by no means the only avenue through which the frustrations of factory-life may be partially eased. There are innocent escapes, like day-dreaming and the football pools. There are also more violent solutions. One of these is little-documented, but, I suspect, significant. It consists of individual sabotage. A worker who is hard-pressed by the speed of his machine may find a way to cause it to stop. The first time I observed this happening I was a boy in a colliery in the Midlands. I was sent to a conveyor-head on the coal-face which was rather difficult to operate, since the seam through which the face was running was very thin and rather badly faulted. I arrived to find a lad sitting by the gear-head, wielding a seven-pound hammer. He had stopped the belt from running, and was carefully whacking at the metal stitches which joined two long sections of belt together. Raw, I asked him what he was doing. 'Won't that break the belt?' I said. 'What the hell do you think I'm trying to do?' he replied. When the conveyor in this seam broke, it did not assure lads like this belt-driver of an easy time. Far from it. They had to race about up and down the face, snaking on their bellies all the way, and working much harder than usual The boy was registering his protest against boredom, he was getting some of his own back on the machine which dominated him, and he was demonstrating his indispensability to the colliers down the face who normally took his efforts for granted.

In all these integrated protests the psychologists who study small group behaviour might labour for months to find a co-ordinated pattern of response. But there is one central question which needs to be asked: why did he not contemplate the feelings of the manager who was striving to raise output, or of the Coal Board who were currently trying to beat a fuel crisis of major proportions, or of a government which was trying against odds to restore a shattered economy which still rested on coal? To ask it is to dismiss it. It is safe to say that these important matters never even entered his head. Why should they? Who could truthfully say that they were problems in which he had even a fractional interest? By sabotaging all these worthy drives, this one boy was making his own life more difficult, but more interesting. Doubtless a delinquent solution. But how many millions of such delinquent incidents are there every day in British industry? Sabotage of this kind, it should be emphasised, is purely an individual reaction. There have been times when sabotage has been used as a collective, trade union, weapon: notably the Luddite episode. It was an integral weapon in the syndicalist arsenal, both in the shape of temporary or permanent disablement of machines, in the broadcasting of discreditable commercial secrets, and in the practice of ca'canny and obstructionism. But in his book, *Strikes,* G. C. K. Knowles argues, rather convincingly, that it 'generally characterises a weak trade union movement, where… it is difficult to prevent the use of blacklegs or to maintain a long strike'.[11]

Paradoxically, a principal obstacle to personal withdrawal of these kinds is precisely the development of solidarity among the workers. This also takes place as a reflex response to their treatment in this alienated environment. Not only do the loyalties which workers form to one another greatly reduce absenteeism and increase the degree of attention paid to mutual tasks and safety, but often men have found ways to relate themselves to what they have rightly regarded as a hostile society, precisely through the institutions which they have formed to protect themselves from it. If one examines the progress of such fierce rebels as Ben Tillett, John Burns, Ernest Bevin, and Ray Gunter, from subversive fire-raisers and rabble-rousers to establishmentarian reconcilers, dousers of conflict, disseminators of official pieties, one can quickly see that it has only taken place through the medium of solidary opposition, which has been contained within the hostile social structure. Unions have formed not only a front-line defence against the regime of alienation and exploitation, but also a bridge from the condition of withdrawal to 'involvement' in a controlled way in the policing, for Authority, of what is for it a fundamentally lawless territory. They are thus inherently ambivalent.

During the early years of the postwar boom, which effectively disoriented a whole generation of leading socialist propagandists, it was popular to assume that the attainment of full employment had solved all the basic problems which have been traditionally posed in socialist discussion. As C. A. R. Crosland has put it:

> 'The status of the worker, in any sense, has been rather substantially enhanced as a result of full employment, rising real wages, social security legislation and a general change in the social climate...'[12]

Within this view of things, not only had poverty been dissolved, but 'democracy and social justice' were on their way. For Crosland, the principal significance of the problems we have been discussing would be the evidence that they offer of lack of 'job satisfaction'. He would tackle them on two levels: on the low range by 'improving the standard of personnel management,' and as a longer-range goal by 'unravelling the natural group relationships' at work in order to 'align these with the technological necessities of the work process'. This bizarre devaluation of the problem is a classic example of what Marx would have denounced as 'commodity-fetishism'. Rather than align technique with human needs, Crosland's crude and philistine approach is inevitably the reverse; it does not envisage for one moment a *human* society in which things serve people. But even Crosland is prepared to admit the historical concern of socialism with this goal:

'Historically, the aspiration towards a "juster" organisation of industry has been enshrined in the demand for industrial democracy and workers' control. This has a long history in the Labour Movement... reaching a climax in the stormy decade before the First World War when even revolutionary syndicalism briefly caught the imagination of the British unions; while Guild Socialism, a more prudent and pacific version, took a strong hold on the minds of younger socialist writers...'[13]

However, Crosland by no means infers from this that 'justice' might require that attention be paid to these pioneers: on the contrary:

'If we wish to revive this issue, we shall not derive much help from the old literature... (it) was ideologically rooted in a theory of "wage slavery" *which has no relevance to present-day conditions.*'[14] (my italics)

It is in the light of this comfortable conviction that much of the debate which has troubled academic sociology, concerning affluence and the changing class structure, has been conducted and as a result has been incapable of revealing much more than surface platitudes. 'A washing machine is a washing machine is a washing machine,' David Lockwood has written. His words might with profit be branded upon the rumps of most psephologists and a good many political commentators.

The relationships between employer and worker which the first Guild Socialists described as 'the bondage of wagery' has not in the least been ameliorated by motor cars and refrigerators. On the contrary. While no one would deny that there has been an absolute improvement in the standards of living of workers in all the advanced capitalist countries, which has continued throughout most of the past two decades (and which has only been arrested during the epoch of advanced, modernising technical innovation inaugurated by Crosland and his colleagues when they assumed political office), the important thing is that this absolute improvement has not been accompanied by any significant *relative* improvement in the rewards of Labour as opposed to those of Capital. What really matters in evaluating this situation is not simply the yardstick of comparative consumption, which is often misleading. The key to an understanding of the psychology of industry is the yardstick of comparative *accumulation*, or agglomeration of *power.*

The original Marxist conception of exploitation never concerned simple money robbery; it always involved itself with the alienation of the product of labour from the control of the labourer, in which workers produce, over and above their own livelihoods *at whatever level of 'affluence'*, a volume of capital, which, under alien direction, concentrates ever greater economic force against them in ever fewer hands. Conceived in these terms, 'exploitation' has been continuously intensified and aggravated throughout the whole history of capitalism.[15] The growth of scale of modern industry is clearly conjoined with the distillation of corporate political and social power, which has not been diminished in any way by 'high', or near-full employment, wage-levels. Decision-takers, deriving steadily augmented authority from direct and indirect titles to capital, cluster in a tightening throng at one pole of society; at the other pole are massed the vassals, who, in spite of the fog of a vast ballyhoo of cynical devices for 'participation' or 'involvement', feel the continuous pressure of attempts to cut back, erode and remove any traces of real rights which they may have been able to grasp at their own immediate level, over the shaping of their own tasks and direction. Of course trade unions have been able to seize some serious powers at the workshop level, over working arrangements and the disposition of the labour force, during the intensive competition for labour which has persisted for most of the postwar period.[16] But these powers, of which shop stewards are rightly jealous, are under constant fire from authority, both in management and the State at large. And while it would be quite wrong to minimise the strength and self-confidence of the trade unions in this persistent struggle, it would be absurd to overlook the fragmentation which has been induced in their ranks by the same economic and political processes. If they were consciously bent upon the destruction of the power of capital, the trade unions could find means to accomplish it: this no one doubts. But within the higgling of contending interests inside the present power-structure it seems absurd to speak of 'trade union power' in the same breath as the power of capital. In the past few years the monolithic National Union of Mineworkers, with near thirty members of parliament, including a number of ministers, and under a Labour government upon which it has a thousand claims and ties, has found it impossible to secure the fulfilment of the wholly specific promises it had been given before victory in the elections. A sympathetic Minister of Power recently burst into tears at a confrontation between trade union and government spokesmen, but grim and implacable behind him sat Mr. Douglas Jay, the voice of the Treasury and the bankers.[17] When all the miners in the land weigh less than a handful of bankers, it is premature to assume the rout of management prerogatives.

Both C. A. R. Crosland and H. A. Clegg, who have in numerous books and articles celebrated the virtues of permanent trade union oppositional power, have during the Wilson administration been lending every possible practical assistance to the crusade to roll these powers back.[18] The inconsistency in their behaviour reflects a deeper inconsistency in their ideas. These ideas found a popular expression in Michael Shanks's account, *The Stagnant Society*, which was, in the terms of this kind of literature, a bestseller. In retrospect it may be thought that Shanks not only puts a key part of the Crosland-Clegg view into a nutshell, but also provides a convenient epitome of the basic industrial relations assumptions of the Labour government:

'There is no greater morale booster for a worker than the feeling that he too is consulted on policy questions and plays his part in influencing managerial decisions. Of course, in any form of democracy there is an element of humbug. Our rulers never, in fact, allow us as much power as they pretend to. The sovereign people can only be permitted to exercise its power on certain limited occasions and within certain defined limits – otherwise the operations of government would be paralysed. Nevertheless, the illusion of power is good for us, besides imposing important restrictions on our rulers.

This applies to industrial democracy, where the element of make-believe must of necessity be greater than in political democracies. Because of the highly technical nature of the decisions which have to be taken, the management must retain ultimate control of the policy. Moreover, the analogy which is often drawn between industrial and political democracy breaks down on two vital points. The first is over the diversity of aims. Ultimately, we all have a common interest in the survival of our political community. But in a factory this may not be so. Only the employer has an interest in preserving the factory at all costs – and even he may be anxious to sell out. But the workers' interests might well be best served by increasing wages and decreasing hours of work to the point where the concern might be driven bankrupt – provided there were other jobs in the district for them to go to.

This brings us to the second reason why industrial democracy cannot be equivalent to political democracy. The political rights of the individual in society derive largely from the fact that he is compelled to live in it. But the worker in industry can always 'vote with his feet' by moving to another factory. The unit of society, in other words, is not all embracing. This means that the worker cannot with justice claim the same rights *vis-à-vis* his employer as he can as a citizen *vis-à-vis* his government.

Industrial democracy, in other words, is a matter of tactics rather than of high principle. It is in no sense immoral to run one's business as a rigid autocracy – but it is probably foolish. It is equally foolish, however, to surrender one's ultimate power of decision to a group of workers, or even to all the workers. Industrial democracy cannot be like a two-party political democracy, in which today's opposition may be tomorrow's government. In industrial democracy a permanent administration confronts a permanent opposition – and as everybody knows, in parliamentary terms this is a most healthy situation. To look at this matter sensibly, we would do well to forget all about the mother of parliaments and the far-flung analogies of the pundits, and consider the issue on its merits.

If one is to talk sensibly of industrial democracy then the first thing is to deflate it and empty it of ideology. It is the fact and not the form of consultation that matters.'[19]

Of course, in this passage, Shanks ducks all the main problems. He outflanks his opponents by a simple device: he narrows the base of his model of industrial democracy to the point where it becomes possible to derive a whole series of completely discrepant analogies. The real unit which socialists aspire to democratise is not, as he is claiming, the factory. It is the economy. If it is true to say that members of a factory can 'vote with their feet', and most of us would claim that that was only true within very straitened limits, then the proper answer to this is that within his own analogy people who don't like Wapping can go to Broadstairs. (With similar difficulties, be it added.) The moment one begins to argue about 'society' the parallel area of dispute becomes the economy. It is absurd to pretend that members of 'the economy' can leave *it* any more easily than they can leave 'society'. If the State marks out the frontiers of 'society', then, to be sure, it is easier by far to leave society than the economy, for the very good and simple reason that not the State but the market marks out the shape of economic frontiers. In this case the reverse of Shanks's argument is true: it is far more easy for English feet to vote for Australia or Japan than to vote their way out of the economy. To argue for democratic control of the economy is not to argue against factory democracy: factories could and should be democratically administered. But to establish norms of workshop democracy in an uncontrolled and undemocratic economy is to conduct a permanent Canute-like dialogue with the ocean of the market. Sometimes the tide will conform to our desires. The important times are those when it does not. Every day, mild fluctuations in demand wreak havoc in existing traditions of factory organisation. It is only if the economy at large is *both* planned and democratised, that the extension of democratic forms to the workshops has any permanency. As far as the Shanks argument is concerned, factory democracy can be vulgarly related to democratic central planning much in the same way that, within his own inadequate analogy, local government might be related to national government.

More woefully ill-founded though is Shanks's conviction that, in the sense that the opposition can never be allowed to win, there can be no two-party democracy within an industrial democracy. If the controllers of an economic plan are democratically controlled, they must be subject to organised criticism, backed by a free press and the liberal standards of open comment. If they are so subject, the possibility cannot be excluded that they might be displaced. In any of the existing centrally planned economies one cares to think of, it is fairly plausible to assume that some, at least, of the planners *would* be displaced if effective popular controls of this kind were established. Whether a democratic plan would necessarily require two or more institutionally established parties it is difficult to say in advance: no such plan exists as a convenient model. Probably its norms would require more of an unleashing of shifting but articulate caucuses and lobbies, forming and reforming according to the emergence of new social needs and pressures. These themselves would engender successive controversies and then settle them as they arose. But none of this is what Shanks is talking about, I will be told. Precisely. When he appeals for this whole problem to 'be deflated and emptied of ideology', those reading him might be tempted to offer a quiet 'Amen'. The fact, is that his whole assumption, that 'a permanent administration confronts a permanent opposition' in this best of all possible worlds, is completely ideological, in the precise traditional meaning of the word. *Why* can our industrial controllers never be displaced by popular vote when their policies cause disquiet? Because they are appointed to and fixed in their positions by the institution of property. Property alone within the structure can displace them, yet it is so much of a taboo that in this vital discussion it cannot even be mentioned. Every single form of rebuttal of democratic arguments which is now being deployed against trade unionists demanding real extensions of industrial democracy could equally have been, and indeed probably was, invoked by the squirearchy in its staunch resistance to the most elementary democratic demands within the political field.

This complex of arguments forms a pattern. The orthodox 'revisionist' critics of socialism (who have captured at any rate the industrial relations policies of the Labour government) have been from the beginning prepared to recognise widespread alienation, which they have seen purely as a psychological condition, a form of individual withdrawal.

They have indeed been prepared to appropriate as their own the call to 'radically improve the status' of the working population, and to 'transform the quality of industrial life'. But they have diagnosed the condition simply as a response to modern technologies, without seriously considering how such technologies came to be enforced, and what conditioned their employment. It has always been assumed by them that it is 'natural' for people to adapt to the requirements of the market in this field. In the words of Brecht, their failure has been a refusal to

> *Inquire if a thing be necessary:*
> *Especially if it is common.*

Had they been able to do this, they might have even gone on to learn

> *When a thing continually occurs*
> *Not on that account to find it 'natural'.*

Implicitly accepting an impermissible framework for their judgements, they can only seek limited solutions to global problems. They are, for instance, prepared to explore all kinds of experiments in factory group dynamics, in order to adjust workers' errant minds to the mechanical imperatives against which they rebel.[20] Just as social psychologists during the war were able to employ group discussion techniques in order to brainwash housewives into feeding their husbands with offal, so this school of thinkers posits a labour force realigned, in small chunks, to a severe appreciation of the need for more production and its own self-abnegation. This is what Crosland means by 'alignment with the technological necessities of the work-process'. To help sell this placebo, labels like 'industrial democracy' can be applied to it. As Shanks revealingly confesses, this involves multiplying 'humbug' by 'make-believe'. But there is a limit to the potency of group manipulation, and the problem, truly posed, has never been one of how people may adapt to machines in the abstract. It has been one of adapting to *someone's* machines.

To explore what this means, consider two greenhouses. One, in a back garden, contains a happy fanatic who saved money to build it and now spends every spare minute nourishing tomatoes which he could possibly buy cheaper in the market. While he is in this greenhouse, this man would probably describe himself as 'free'. Yet he is certainly 'working'. The other greenhouse is one of a long row in a nursery. Two labourers pass on the way into adjoining doors. 'Roll on Friday' we hear them saying. Our particular man enters his workplace where we observe that, after carefully scanning around him, he settles comfortably down, and falls to the reading of the *Daily Mirror*. He is not working, but he is 'at work', and would certainly prefer to be reading the *Daily Mirror* elsewhere. He is behaving in an alienated manner. But can we say that greenhouses are alienating? Of course not: our first man cannot spend long enough in them. He is his own master. The other two are working for someone else. Ignore this simple fact at peril: for the whole essence of the alienation we have been describing is that property, the private control of public resources, is at the heart of it. Of course, greenhouses can be personal belongings. In this they differ from, say, a four-million pound production-line in a vehicle factory which can never, for any of its individual operatives, become really 'my' machine. But such a costly complex *could* become 'our' machine, and if it did, this would merely bring the juridical norm into line with what has long been a social need. Until this happens, every factory is a flagrant assault on the categorical imperative: 'I ought never to act except in such a way that I can also will that my maxim should become a universal law.' If those words were to be enforced in any working enterprise for half an hour, it would cease to function altogether. Socialist revolutions in full flood apart, capitalist industry is the most sustained and awe-inspiring collective effort which men have ever made: yet its ethos is such that members of the collective only traditionally use the words 'we' and 'us' when they are making hostile demands upon its directors.

None of this is to say that all forms of work will become pleasant once we nationalise the means of production, distribution and exchange. The contrary: their very unpleasantness, in a really open democracy, will hasten the social effort to abolish them. The effort to do this has always been seen by socialists as involving a double on-slaught: efforts must be made to plan a technological explosion, capable of blasting out continuous all-round cuts in working hours; at the same time there must also be a systematic transfer of increasing ranges of consumer goods to welfare forms of distribution, gradually but remorselessly replacing money as the normal means of personal transactions, and increasingly relegating it to the role of an accounting device between various public corporations. The effect of these onslaughts would be a vast increase in *free time,* which, in such conditions, as Marx frequently pointed out, 'is the *most productive* time of all'. This, in turn, would lethally undermine the division of labour itself, which has hitherto given rise not only to the impositions of class and rank, but also to the conditions which Ruskin so tellingly described:

'We have much studied and perfected, of late, the great civilised invention of the division of labour; only we give it a false name. It is not, truly speaking, the labour that is divided; but the men: divided into mere seg-ments of men – broken into small fragments and crumbs of life; so that all the little piece of intelligence that is left in a man is not enough to make a pin, or a nail, but exhausts itself in making the point of a pin, or the head of a nail. Now it is a good and desirable thing, truly, to make many pins in a day; but if we could only see with what crystal sand their points were polished – sand of human soul, much to be magnified before it can be discerned for what it is – we should think there might be some loss in it also. And the great cry that rises from all our manufacturing cities, louder than the furnace blast, is all in very deed for this – that we manufacture everything there except men; we blanch cotton, and strengthen steel, and refine sugar, and shape pottery; but to brighten, to strengthen, to refine or to form a single living spirit, never enters into our estimate of advantages.'[21]

Ruskin may have approached this terrible reality in a one-sided manner, but at least he faced it. Our present generation of 'socialist' leaders do not even know what it is about. They may have thought about it, briefly, once; and in mitigation we can accept that to deal with it no doubt requires a fairly long-range strategy. They are all busy people. However, not thinking about these long-range problems makes the range still longer, and the haul uphill still harder.

By foreshortening its range and lowering its aim, Labour in Britain has set a cruel trap for itself. Immediate, 'practical' problems have for so long dominated the minds of the Labour establishment that they have no independent criteria by which to respond to them. No one in the present government has time to think about the overcoming of the division of labour. But if no one thinks about such matters then the goals of the movement become devalued. For all the loud noises we have had from Labour leaders about 'equality' over the past fifteen years, every evidence appears to show that this notion is strictly limited to piety of a most abstract kind. The complete failure of any prominent spokesman of the Labour Party to discuss this kind of problem in fundamental terms, during the whole of the past two decades, reveals a definitive retreat from the most crucial front in the battle for Labour's aims.

This refusal to think about these ultimate problems blocks Labour leaders from opening up the vision of the members of the movement. At the same time it forces them to accommodate to a position in which their short-range moves are completely blind. They come to rely entirely on the given priorities of the established system. And so, they come to reduce all political choices to administrative alternatives. In this way, the 1964 Labour government found itself with the strategic aim of 'restoring the economy'; after which (in some way which has neither been specified nor, one suspects, agreed) 'we will pay ourselves a dividend'.[22] Instead of becoming the reason for beginning to create a new one, the difficulties of the old economic order became a pretext for placing in jeopardy even the limited programme of amelioration which had previously been envisaged. Not only has the incidence of poverty been increasing, but there are signs that this is happening at an accelerated rate. Professor Townsend, who calculated recently that some 7 million people were living at or below the standard available on National Assistance, is now publicly speculating about the increase of this figure by another million. In this serious condition, the policies of retrenchment which have been imposed upon the administration add their own quota of misery. The deliberate creation of artificial unemployment, referred to under the repulsive name of 'shake-out', marks out the ultimate capitulation to the logic of the market, to the primacy of property over all humane interests.

A man's hopes are his moral boundaries. He will rarely press beyond them. If someone merely aspires to put a new roof on his kitchen, not only is it easier to fulfil this dream than to bring about a world in which *every* cook may learn to govern the State, but, when the roof is on, you will not find prime ministers in the kitchen by accident. In the event, in 1964, even the kitchen roof could not be seen to. Worse. Having accepted the administrative priorities, the restoration of the old order to good health required the new ministers to make incisions in the economic body. Cuts could not be inflicted upon capital's prerogatives without stepping outside the administrative routine which had by now become more demanding with each submission made to it. And so arose the need for first piece-meal, and then wholesale attacks on the living standards and liberties of the very people the Government had been elected to protect.

The word for this is 'betrayal'. It is an emotive word, but, unfortunately, it is accurate. Yet the first and fundamental betrayal took place a while ago, almost unnoticed: it was a betrayal of socialist theory, since which the events of 1964 and onwards have only made manifest something which was gestating, latent in a small flow of books and articles, for a decade and half before.

Having inherited the leadership of a vast mass organisation of working people, the present dominant caucus had not the remotest idea of an aim for the whole complex. Because their horizons were so limited, they reacted like any sealed-in provincial village community, and embellished their own immediate social arrangements with polite and decorous descriptions to soften the realities. In the village everyone will tell you that much can be improved, that no one is complacent, that many reforms are needed, and so on. Similarly Mr. Crosland was in favour of uplifting the status of the workers, just as Mr. Shanks would spread more widely the humbug of democracy, just as all the world and especially Mr. Harold Wilson would love to blow warm blasts of modernising wind through every enterprise. But workers are not merely deprived of status by some genteel scale. They are, as every line of this essay is meant to argue, wage slaves. There can, if this is true, be no easy continual uplift of the people without a fundamental structural change in society as a whole. A wage slave does not cease to be a wage slave when he can buy a refrigerator. Roman slaves might be thin or fat, sad or cheerful, employed to entertain their masters' lions as dinner or their masters' wives as lovers; wage slaves too come in all sizes and conditions. Some even drive to work in motor cars. As they trod the grape harvest, the Roman slaves on the *latifundiae* probably ate some too. You cannot tell a wage slave by his looks. You can tell him by the fact that on Monday he says 'Roll on Friday'. He is defined by the fact that he lives in little islands of freedom called 'leisure'.

That these, to an outsider, may be more and more coming to resemble the surrounding sea of 'work' is not so surprising. It is hard to be a five-day slave, free at weekends. Recently in the same week, I visited a pharmaceutical factory employing some thousands of girls, and a fun-arcade at Skegness. In both places, rows and rows of girls stood poring over rows and rows of little machines. The first enterprise was for bottling, sealing, and labelling pills; engaged in it the girls were 'producing'. At the second, which was for taking away the sixpences earned in the first, the operatives were 'consuming'. Work and leisure, production and consumption: fully *human* beings would have to reason with subtlety to discover the difference. Wage slaves know it intimately; it is the first fact of their existence. If wage slaves who earn above average pay feel the freer for that on Friday night, they will most probably feel all the more enslaved on Monday morning. A Derbyshire colliery under-official won £20,000 on the football pools two years ago, and having assembled a fair-sized crowd in the pityard, he ceremonially burnt his pit-clothes in front of them. They knew what he meant.

* * *

In sum, if slavery is a social relationship and not an absolute level of distress; and if slavery may be discovered wherever the will of one man is involuntarily and arbitrarily subordinated to that of another; then we remain bound to the same basic problems which the Labour Movement faced, one hundred years ago, when Marx offered it this excellent advice:

> 'At the same time (that they defend themselves with vigour in all partial battles for improved conditions) ... the working class ought not to exaggerate to themselves the ultimate working of these everyday struggles. They ought not to forget that they are fighting with effects, but not with the causes of those effects; that they are retarding the downward movement, but not changing its direction; that they are applying palliatives, not curing the malady. They ought, therefore, not to be exclusively absorbed in these unavoidable guerrilla fights incessantly springing up from the never-ceasing encroachments of capital or changes in the market. They ought to understand that, with all the miseries it imposes on them, the present system simultaneously engenders the material conditions and the social forms necessary for an economic reconstruction of society. Instead of the *conservative* motto: "A fair day's wages for a fair day's work!" they ought to inscribe upon their banners the *revolutionary* watchword 'For the abolition of the wages system!'[23]

First published in 1967

Footnotes

1. A. Barratt Brown, *The Machine and the Worker* (London, 1934), p.85.
2. ibid.
3. ibid. p.86.
4. R. M. Fox, *The Triumphant Machine* (London, 1928), p.35.
5. D. J. (Dennis Johnson), 'Factory Time' in *New Left Review*, 31(1965), pp.51-7.
6. Herman Melville, *The Tartarus of Maids* in Collected Short Stories (London, 1950).
7. Norbert Wiener, *The Human Use of Human Beings* (Boston, 1950).
8. An honoured place among these toilers will be reserved for Harold

Wilson, who will need a fair slab of eternity to demonstrate how easily he could dispense with 'conservatism' on the shop floor in order to boost the dynamism of British Industry. It is perhaps unfair to predict that Purgatorial Industry may also slacken its pace when it comes under his inspired tutelage.

9. 'The Sick Society', Dr. Beric Wright, in the *Director* (October 1966), pp.90-1.

10. ibid, p.92. For an account of the Report of the Institute's Medical Centre see the *Director* (May 1966), p.270ff.

11. G. C. K. Knowles, *Strikes* (Oxford, 1952), p.13. The best known advocate of sabotage as a trade union weapon in this country was William Mellor, cf. the appropriate chapter in *Direct Action* (1920). Recently the idea has been discussed in the militant journal *Solidarity* in somewhat similar terms. Since this essay was written a major study of *Sabotage* has been written by Geoff Brown (Spokesman Books, 1977).

12. C. A. R. Crosland, 'What Does the Worker Want?' in *Encounter* (February 1959), p.10.

13. Crosland, *The Future of Socialism* (London, 1956), p.343.

14. ibid, pp.343-4.

15. Those who doubt this interpretation of Marx should carefully re-read *Wage Labour and Capital*. An extract may serve to point his attitude both in the field of consumption and accumulation:

'A house may be large or small; as long as the surrounding houses are equally small it satisfies all social demands for a dwelling. But if a palace arises beside the little house, the little house shrinks into a hut. The little house shows now that its owner has only very slight or no demands to make: and however high it may shoot up in the course of civilisation, if the neighbouring palace grows to an equal or even greater extent, the dweller in the relatively small house will feel more and more uncomfortable, dissatisfied and cramped within its four walls.

'A noticeable increase in wages presupposes a rapid growth of productive capital. The rapid growth of productive capital brings about an equally rapid growth of wealth, luxury, social needs, social enjoyments. Thus, although the enjoyments of the worker have risen, the social satisfaction they give has fallen in comparison with the increased enjoyments of the capitalists, which are inaccessible to the worker, in comparison with the state of the development of society in general. Our needs and enjoyments spring from society; we measure them, therefore, by society and not by the objects of their satisfaction. Because they are of a social nature, they are of a relative nature...

'Real wages may remain the same, may even rise, and yet relative wages fall ... If, therefore, the income of the worker increases with the rapid growth of capital, the social gulf that separates the worker from the capitalist increases at the same time, the power of capital over labour, the dependence of labour on capital, increases at the same time.' from *Selected Works* (London, 1945), vol. 1, pp.268-73.

16. For a balanced treatment of this, see Tony Topham, 'Shop Stewards and Workers' Control' in *New Left Review*, 25 (May. June 1964), pp.3-16.

17. cf. *The Scottish Miner* (February 1966).

18. Compare Clegg's discussion of these matters in *A New Approach to Industrial Democracy* (Oxford, 1960) with his part in framing the Devlin and Pearson Reports on the decasualisation of dock workers (Cmd 2734, August 1965) and on the Seamen's Wage Claim (Cmd 3025, June 1966).

19. Michael Shanks, *The Stagnant Society* (London, 1961), p.160.

20. Crosland, 'What Does the Worker Want?' loc. cit., pp.16-17.

21. Ruskin, *The Stones of Venice*, Section II, chapter vi.

22. As James Callaghan pointed out to the Fabians at a gathering during the 1963 TUC: 'A Labour government must not rush its fences... its first job must be to get industry moving again (!). Then, we can start paying ourselves a dividend' (*Guardian*, 4 September 1963).

23. Karl Marx, 'Value Price and Profit' in *Selected Works*, vol. 1 (London, 1945), p.337.

4

Forming the
Institute for Workers' Control

The Institute for Workers' Control had launched itself in 1968, with an exciting keynote speech from the victorious candidate in the Engineers' Presidential Election. This was published, alongside this paper, in the Bulletin of the new Institute, which was also founded in 1968. The Bulletin of the Institute was established immediately after its foundation in March 1968, firstly as a quarterly journal under my editorship. This task was subsequently taken over by Tony Topham, and then by Michael Barratt Brown. Finally it became, with the tenth number in 1973, the task of Stephen Bodington and John Jennings, who converted it into a fortnightly newsletter and discussion journal. Among the regular contributors were: Richard Fletcher, Walt Greendale, Eric Heffer, John Hughes, Walter Kendall, Brian Nicholson, Ernie Roberts and Audrey Wise.

Hugh Scanlon was only one of the new union leaders who gave their support to the Institute. A strong phalanx of miners, including Lawrence Daly, Peter Heathfield and Jack Dunn were also regularly to be seen at the Institute's conferences. Jack Dunn served on the Institute's Council. From the Transport and General Workers' Union came the Institute's new President, Bill Jones, later to be elected as President of his own Union, and member of the General Council of the TUC. A galaxy of other notables from the T&GWU included dockers' leaders Walter Greendale and Brian Nicholson, busmen's leader Jack Ashworth, and representatives from the motor industry. The Union's research officer, Fred Silberman, played an active role, as did his colleague Regan Scott.

The movement towards workers' control took a big step forward at the end of March, with the Sixth Conference on Workers' Control at Nottingham University. Previous gatherings on the same theme have been held, under the auspices of the trade union newspaper, *Voice of the Unions*, the Centre for Socialist Education, and, on one occasion, the London Co-operative Society. Beginning in 1964, with a gathering of some eighty academics, socialist journalists, and a handful of trade unionists, the discussion on industrial democracy has widened out to the point where, this year, at Nottingham, five hundred delegates, mostly from trade union branches and shop stewards' committees, but some representing their national trade union executives, met in twenty seminar groups to consider detailed projects for their industries, and in plenary session, to discuss the development of an overall strategy for the trade union movement as a whole.

Of course, from the original meeting onwards, there has been a steadily increasing volume of interest in the issue of workers' control: it has preoccupied the Liberal Party's Youth Movement for two or three years now, and, at the same time, it has provoked the Labour Party National Executive to establish a study-group which, under the tutelage of such committed industrial democrats as John Hughes, Bill Wedderburn and Jack Jones, has produced a report which goes further in advocating the extension of trade union powers than any other similar document for a great many years. The fact that a Labour government is driving at full speed in the opposite direction to that indicated in the report does not in the least minimise its importance: with all its numerous faults, it provides, at the very least, a convenient measure by which trade unions activists can judge the extent of the default of the government which they have levered into office.

But, even though the major political parties of erstwhile radicalism have been dragged into this crucial argument, and even though some of *the* major trade unions have begun to discuss the problems of democracy with a quite new enthusiasm during the past few years, at no point has the discussion been taken further than at the Workers' Control Conferences themselves. They have commenced to provide a whole stream of arguments and projects which can begin to serve to take the issue out of the realm of general pieties, into the field of immediately practical options for the whole trade union Left.

Indeed, the trade unions have felt the impact of these programmes directly and immediately. For instance, the second and third Workers' Control Conferences, which were held in 1965 in London and Manchester respectively, brought together a group of steel-workers from Sheffield and other areas (notably Scunthorpe) who were able to agree upon a whole series of recommendations as to how workers' control should be applied to the nationalised steel industry. These suggestions were carefully discussed by the influential craftsmen's unions, which agreed to adopt them as official policy: so 'that the government's shifty measures for conjuring up some semblance of the forms of industrial democracy without any of its content, which were pushed through into law by Mr. Richard Marsh (in order, as the *Director* hunched editorially, to 'involve the workers' representatives in accepting responsibility for some of the unpopular decisions which will have to be taken') are now confronted by coherent alternative plans with the full support of a major trade union body.

Or again, from the first Conference onwards, agreement was reached that a central, even crucial, workers' control demand was that for industrial and social accountability: and the slogan 'open the books' was carried out from the 1964 gathering, small though it was, to strike deep roots in the unions. It was as 'a result of the campaign around this war-cry that the National Union of Seamen, in the middle of its 1966 strike, published its reply to the Pearson Enquiry, entitled *Not Wanted on Voyage*, which turned around the recognition of the fact that the totally unjustifiable degree of business secrecy which protects the shipowners from 'having to reveal in public any worthwhile information about key sectors of their profits and reserves, meant that Lord Pearson's very learned team had no conceivable means of knowing whether the shipowners could afford to meet the men's claim or not. Numerous other unions have since adopted the same strategic call.

In short, from the beginning these discussions have established a dialogue in which workpeople and academics, trade union activists and technical specialists, students and union leaders, have been able to meet and test out ideas on one another. The growth of the *Voice* newspapers has been a key part of this dialogue, which has now, with the election of Mr. Hugh Scanlon to the Presidency of the Amalgamated Engineers and Foundryworkers' Union, begun to assume considerable institutional importance. Naturally, workers' control ideas have always had their partisans in the union offices: and recently, the work of Jack and Bill Jones in the Transport & General Workers' Union, or of the late Dave Lambert of the Foundryworkers' Union, or of the Public Employees' secretary Sid Hill, has made a notable contribution to the growth of the explicit movement for control. But the election of Hugh Scanlon marks out a new stage in the campaign, because he fought a crucial election as a dedicated proponent of workers' control, and was widely identified as a crusader for these ideals, to the considerable public distress of his major opponents in the union.

As a founder of *Engineers' Voice,* and a principal speaker at last year's Coventry Conference on workers' control, he had, long before the Nottingham Conference, made important contributions to the discussion. But this was his first public appearence on a workers' control platform since his victory in the AEF election, so that naturally his speech was awaited with some curiosity and eagerness. It was not disappointing. Indeed, there is some ground for saying that it was the most comprehensive and compelling statement of the arguments for industrial democracy, and the most far-sighted attempt to think in overall strategic terms, that has been made by any British Trade Union leader for perhaps fifty years.

Keenly aware of the traditional roots of the movement, Scanlon traced its continuity back to the syndicalist upheaval before the First World War, the publication of *The Miners' Next Step* in the South Wales coalfield, and the subsequent upsurge of the shop stewards' movement in the engineering industry itself. He went on to explain how the inter-war depression and its long postwar hangover in trade union thinking, produced a largely defensive mentality in the higher councils of the trade union movement. Yet now all this was changing, and he was anything but pessimistic about the possibilities, even given due understanding of the very real pressures which are being exerted on the trade unions by the establishment in all its guises. For workers are becoming increasingly prone to question, and to reject, managerial prerogatives, both in defence of their own immediate interests, but also as a result of growing technological expertise, and the outcome of the educational and technical demands made upon the work people by industry itself.

In this context, Scanlon saw a need for a joint offensive to be mounted: in private industry to extend the area of trade union rights; and in publicly owned industry to establish the direct control (not, he said, in a withering aside, 'participation' in other peoples' decisions) of all the associated production, managerial and technical workers over the decision-taking machinery which affects their working lives. He spelt this all out in great detail in his demands for the steel industry, closely following the proposals which had already emerged in the steelworkers' discussions over the past years.

'The National Craftsmen's Co-ordinating Committee for the Iron and Steel Industry has submitted detailed proposals. Thus, at the Combine or group level it is proposed that the appointment of a head for the Operating Board should be subject to ratification by a Group Workers' Council. These Workers' Councils, according to the N.C.C.C. proposal, should be elected on a half and half basis from the appropriate trade unions and from shop, mill or office committees, and they should have the power to receive reports on all policies and to ask for detailed costings of all departments. At plant level, both the chairman and management representatives should be ratified by departmental committees or by the Workers' Council, while half the membership should be drawn from elected workers' representatives. At shop, mill and office level, the proposals are even more radical. Indeed they urge that democratically elected committees should subject to ratification the appointment of shop managers and foremen, the deployment of labour, promotion, the hiring and dismissing of workers, safety, welfare and disciplinary matters. They should also have special responsibilities for training and education, and other responsibilities delegated from the combine or Group Workers' Council.

The machinery suggested gives workers and union both the powers of scrutiny and of veto, and so allows for the extension of workers' influence on management beyond the limitations of defensive collective bargaining.'

At the same time, Scanlon also defended trade union independence within such a framework, insisting that the unions had a role to play in defending their members against injustices, and in wage-bargaining, even when the seeds of industrial democracy had taken firm root. He went on to argue for consumer-representation in the process of planning, and concluded with a graphic warning about the dangers of central bureaucracy within national planning, and the need to learn from the mistakes which have been made in the socialist countries by establishing the widest democratic accountability throughout the planning process.

It was a powerful speech, although it was delivered extremely quietly, without any histrionics, deliberatively, as a statement fully considered. The meeting hung on each word, aware that this was a path-breaking statement of the philosophy of a new movement within the mainstream of Labour, not simply an academic paper.

The conference itself worked in something of the same mood. Other important trade union leaders spoke, often tellingly, on the same theme: Ernie Roberts, the Assistant Secretary of the AEF; Ian Mikardo, who besides playing his customary political role, is the President of the Technician's amalgamation, the ASTMS; Bill Jones, the conference chairman, who besides being vice-president of the T&GWU, is the only busman on the General Council of the TUC.

Yet for all the political weight of the platform, it was the seminars which provided the most serious evidence of the developing competence of the new movement: established study groups like those in steel and mining, aircraft and docks, all of which have a large train of publications behind them, and many more to come: and brand new groups, some significantly representative, like that in distribution, or that in agriculture, which had the vice-president of the NUAW as its spokesman; and some frail, but full of ideas, like the six-strong group of young printworkers, or the chemical workers, who had among them a representative from Scott Bader, an established experiment in democratic industrial organisation. A team of technicians reported on the implications of computer technology for industrial democracy, while a huge engineering seminar worked on a lively project to develop alternative demands which could be posed against the package-deal, so often used as a part of employer strategy to whittle down shop stewards' powers. A room full of people were involved in the work of the education seminar, which embraced all the related problems of student power and democracy in the schools. A whole flow of publications can be expected from this group.

Politically, there was a clear division in the Conference between those who saw the struggle for workers' control as being worked out through the existing institutions of the Labour Movement, up to and including the Labour Party itself, and those who were agnostic about possibilities in such fields, and turned towards direct action in various forms. Some people straddled both views. Yet although there was all the potential for heated discussion, had the two views confronted each other on any other ground, in this case the disagreement was by no means disruptive.

First published in 1968

5

A Lame Duck Takes Wing

The summer of 1971 brought the Glasgow shipyards into the centre of the news headlines, when the threat of mass redundancies provoked a powerful response from the workforce, and triggered the famous Upper Clyde Shipbuilders 'work-in'. In the days before this decision was reached, the IWC forwarded to Glasgow two thousand of one of its pamphlets, which concerned a struggle at the Merseyside plants of GEC (General Electric Company), where a workers' takeover had been extensively discussed, but ultimately avoided. The experiences and ideas of the GEC workforce were thus made available to all the shop stewards at Upper Clyde Shipbuilders.

But it was the logic of their situation which persuaded the workers to take the bold step of occupying yards which had come under threat. In this they were strongly encouraged by Tony Benn, who had met the GEC shop stewards before their aborted takeover, and who was sufficiently imaginative to see the electric appeal that the UCS initiative would have.

It was during these days that the IWC met up with Tony Benn, and formed an association which was to ripen into close co-operation. I met with Tony Benn in the earliest days of the UCS takeover, and soon afterwards a small group of IWC Council members visited him at home, in order to share his experiences and their own. Amongst those who took part in this dialogue were Bill Jones, the Institute Chairman, and Ernie Roberts, the Engineers' Assistant General Secretary.

After this meeting, Tony Benn attended the subsequent conference of the Institute, and thenceforward he became a regular participant in its more important meetings.

For me, this exciting episode was to form a friendship which was to become lifelong, undiminished by political disagreements and actually strengthened by the adversities and setbacks which we both encountered in our different battles.

On June 14th, 1971, the British government decided to withhold financial assistance which had been requested by the Directors of

Upper Clyde Shipbuilders, thus allowing the company to go into liquidation. That evening, Tony Benn spoke to the workers' representatives. He was reported next morning in these terms:

'Mr Anthony Wedgwood Benn, shadow spokesman on employment and industry, was loudly cheered at a meeting of Clydeside shop stewards in Clydebank last night when he endorsed the proposed trade union action of "sitting in" in the Upper Clyde Shipbuilding yard threatened with closure.

"This is a decision you have taken and it is for you to decide", said Mr Benn. "Your decision not to evacuate the yard is absolutely justified in the circumstances."

Just as in the case of Rolls Royce, the government had made an appalling blunder over UCS and would have to reverse their course. He had been expecting the news for 12 months, but he did not think the reason given by Mr Davies for the liquidation of UCS stood up to one moment's examination.'[1]

The original suggestion that the workpeople counter dismissals by 'staying put' and working on, had been advanced by Sammy Barr, the convenor of one of the yards constituting the consortium. Apparently it provoked widely different reactions. There were some enthusiasts, but also many voluble sceptics. Yet obviously threatened closures could not sensibly be met by withdrawal of labour, since withdrawal of labour was the precise aim intended by the opposition. Ruling out strike action, more and more workers came to the view that the choice lay between a straightforward sit-in and Sammy Barr's proposals, unless defeat were to be acknowledged from the beginning. A sit-in would need to be maintained for a very long time, judged its opponents. The labour force, recruited from a wide area, scattered around the region, would find it difficult to maintain such an action for weeks, never mind months. But a 'work-in' might, just might, catch people's imaginations and attract that political support, based on a real shift of public opinion, which alone could over-rule a government decision.

During the week after Tony Benn's visit, mass meetings were held in every one of the yards, and the idea of 'working-in' was carried in each of them. A coordinating committee of all the shop stewards in the consortium began to plan to give it reality.

After more than a month of feverish activities by the workers, during which the former Labour Minister of Technology continuously defended their proposals for an occupation of the plant, the government announced, on July 29th, that two of the four UCS yards were to be closed and sold off.

The next day UCS workers seized control of the gates of the threatened John Brown yard, and defied a ban by the recently appointed liquidator on a shop stewards' press conference called within the workplace. At a mass-meeting of the 3,500 workers in the yard, Jimmy Reid, the chairman of the joint co-ordinating committee for the whole UCS consortium, and an AUEW shop steward, reported on the results of the meeting between the stewards and the government at which the work-people had been informed of the proposed closures, which entailed the loss of 6,000 jobs directly, and many thousands more indirectly.

> 'This is the first campaign of its kind in trade unionism', he said. 'We are not going on strike. We are not even having a sit-in. We do not recognise that there should be any redundancies and we are going to "work-in".
>
> We are taking over the yards because we refuse to accept that faceless men can take these decisions. We are not strikers. We are responsible people and we will conduct ourselves with dignity and discipline...There will be no hooliganism, there will be no vandalism, and there will be no bevying.
>
> We are not the wildcats, we want to work. The real wildcats are in Number Ten Downing Street. They are the hardest-faced bunch of political gangsters I have ever met. They make Al Capone and his gunmen look like a troop of Boy Scouts. The biggest mistake we could make is to lie down, capitulate and grovel to them.'[2]

So began the 'work-in' which was to transform the nature of the struggle against unemployment and dismissals in Britain.

There was no affray. Quietly, stewards replaced the gate-man, who simply withdrew on request. Working four-hour rotas, the stewards controlled everything and every person entering or leaving the yards. Consultation with the police revealed that they had no intention of intervening, provided there were no disturbances. The action was to carry on until October 1972, when all four yards involved were saved, and over £47 million of government money committed to the rescue. During the whole time, the organisation developed by the workers remained in full force, in spite of its involvement in a punishing campaign of public relations which became ever more demanding.

The crisis in shipbuilding

Before redundancies were announced in the shipyards, one man in ten in Glasgow's region was already unemployed. Closure of the yards would have created a considerable 'knock-on' effect, taking out jobs in a wide range of ancillary industries which were, to a greater or lesser extent, keyed into shipbuilding.

Shipbuilding in Britain had entered a general crisis. For a decade and a half after the Second World War, things had drifted comfortably: but by 1965 Britain produced only 10% of world shipping, as contrasted with 41% in 1949. The story has, alas, become commonplace. Old, under-capitalised plant in Britain was competing against aggressively managed modern equipment abroad, and, increasingly obviously, it was failing. In 1966 a Government Committee under Lord Geddes reported that British shipyards could not take advantage of the world demand for merchant shipping, because they were both insufficiently specialised and insufficiently concentrated, to develop adequate skills in management, marketing, design, development, purchasing or accounting. Hence the Government of the day intervened, establishing a Shipbuilding Industry Board (SIB) to provide financial aid, and subsequently, through its agency, creating the Upper Clyde Shipbuilders Consortium (UCS) in 1967.[3]

Comprising the new group were: Fairfields, an experiment in joint control involving 50% of Governmental shares and some considerable trade union investment; John Brown's renowned but ramshackle Clydebank yard (with two lesser appendages); Connell's Scotstoun yard; Alexander Stephens' Govan yard, adjoining Fairfields; and Yarrows, an admiralty contractor which soon hived off from UCS after modernising itself under the auspices of the Consortium. As the secretary of the Institute for Workers' Control reported:

'Despite its ambitious conception, the Upper Clyde Shipbuilders Group was launched on very flimsy foundations. The old owners were only too pleased to get out and to receive compensation for doing it. Some of the yards had practically no orders on hand while the others had order books consisting almost entirely of loss-making contracts; these contracts subsequently lost

12 million pounds. On top of this the yards, apart from Govan (Fairfields), were in a state of dilapidation, full of old and out-of-date equipment often badly laid out. To add to the Shipbuilders' (UCS) initial difficulties many of the executives in the former companies continued in office with UCS, brought their old authoritarian methods into the new concern and found it easier to squabble amongst themselves than to co-operate in developing an integrated structure for the new concern.

The first managing director of UCS, A.E. Hepper, a successful stocking manufacturer, added to the burdens of the concern by filling the order books with further loss-making contracts. As a consequence, not only were there no funds available for much needed equipment, but, through an acute shortage of working capital, the company very soon plunged into a serious financial crisis in early 1969. It was only rescued by a loan from the government of 7 million pounds on top of grants of 5 million pounds from the Shipbuilding Industry Board (SIB) and a further 3 million pounds the SIB agreed to subscribe for additional share capital. The Minister of Technology, Anthony Wedgwood Benn, insisted on the introduction of new management and working methods, which involved provision for redundancies. The trade unions accepted these redundancies with great reluctance, but in a situation where general unemployment was not nearly as high as it was soon to become. However, they were able to negotiate higher wage rates as the price for accepting redundancies and new working methods.

A new managing director, Ken Douglas, an experienced and able shipbuilder from Austin Pickergills, was appointed, and he quickly won the support and confidence of the men. He inherited, then, an ill-assorted order book of ships of widely different types and sizes, many of which were still loss-making. Douglas was instrumental in rationalising largely into cargo ships of standard design which allowed for much more straightforward operations. Throughput of steel increased in 1970 from 887 tons per week to an average of 1300 tons the week before the liquidation of UCS was announced; 3 ships were completed in 1968, 12 were launched in 1970 and 15 were expected in 1971. Trading losses had fallen from 12 million pounds to 3 million pounds in a year and profits were confidently expected in 1972. After all the pain and sacrifice the yards were, at last, full of confidence for the future of shipbuilding on the Upper Clyde. The dashing of these expectations was a key factor in the workers' sharp and angry reaction to the government axe after the initial shock and disbelief had passed.'

Why, then, did the government take the decision to cut down UCS just when it was beginning to stand on its own feet? Extracts from a very significant document which throws considerable light on official motivation were published in *The Guardian* in June 1971. The complete text was subsequently released to the public by the shop stewards. It consisted of a letter circulated by Nicholas Ridley to some colleagues in the Conservative Shadow Cabinet in December 1969. Mr Ridley was the Opposition main spokesman on shipbuilding at the time and his report was the result of a brief meeting he had attended with Ken Douglas and a more lengthy conference with Sir Eric Yarrow, who had been hostile to UCS from the outset. Nicholas Ridley recommended that no more government money be given to UCS, particularly as their wage rates were pushing up the rates of the Scott Lithgow Group on the Lower Clyde, and he insisted that a government 'butcher' should be put in to cut up UCS if the Conservatives were returned to power.

John Davies, the Minister of Trade and Industry, had denied all knowledge of the Ridley Report, but nevertheless its author was appointed to a key position in the Department of Trade and Industry by Edward Heath: and thereafter events followed remarkably closely to the pattern laid down in the Ridley document. Ridley himself played a central part in suspending government credit guarantees to shipowners and this was the death blow to the prospects of UCS. It meant that shipowners ceased paying instalments for work completed on ships under construction and that, in turn, UCS were unable to pay their own creditors. As a consequence vital supplies were held back and the work flow was interrupted at a time when the concern was on the point of breaking through to viability. UCS were forced to apply for a further government loan of £6 million in May 1971, but John Davies reaffirmed that no more public money would be given to UCS and that instead a liquidator must be appointed.

'The government was somewhat taken aback by the tremendous outcry against the decision and agreed to appoint a four-man inquiry... (This) reported, after only six weeks of not very intensive work. Their report consisted simply of four pages. It recommended that the Clydebank and Scotstoun yards be run down as current orders were completed and that only the Govan yard (with Stephens yard as an ancillary) be kept open. Even this small concession was barbed: the reprieved yard would operate with a reduced labour force, subject to more intensive discipline and renegotiated wage rates. No arguments or factual documentation were given to support any of these sweeping conclusions. The government refused to publish any such information, without giving any plausible reasons, and despite insistent demands that this be done.

It is perfectly clear that the 'Four Wise Men', as they inevitably came to be known, were under no pressure from the government to offer evidence which might frustrate its own clear intentions. If the workers at UCS were to win any reprieve, they had a fight on their hands, since before they could secure a hearing for their reasoned case, they needed to buy time to delay an imminent execution.'[4]

This was the immediate background to the declaration of the work-in. But things had been stirring in the wider Labour Movement, as well.

A helpful example

The trade union movement learns by experience, and sometimes it learns almost as much from failure as from success. The remarkable successes of the UCS workers were themselves partly attributable to lessons drawn from just such an earlier failure. Contrary to widespread belief, the initiative at UCS was not the first to be taken by the modern movement. The Institute for Workers' Control was formed in 1968, with a view to popularising ideas of industrial democracy. It was first involved in action of this kind in the summer of 1969, when workers at the GEC plants in Liverpool, threatened by factory closures and rationalisations, appealed for its help in providing specialist services and advice to assist a wholesale occupation of Merseyside GEC plants, which were then to be run by a combined shop stewards' committee. Members of the Institute's Council made many visits to Liverpool, and were able to form clear impressions of the difficulties involved in this strategy.[5]

In mid-August, the GEC stewards had announced their plans for a workers' takeover, which, they said, would begin on September 19th. Occupation passes were printed in readiness for the day. There followed a storm of press publicity, which had the merit of popularising (albeit inadvertently) the idea of workers' occupations, among people far removed from Liverpool and its particular problems. At meetings of the stewards, however, it soon became clear, that 'working-in' at GEC was fraught with very great difficulties, and that the management were persistently, and not unskilfully, exploiting these difficulties. Among the questions which workers pressed upon their representatives were a number of recurrent problems.

What, they asked, would happen to the entitlement to redundancy pay of those who took part in the occupation? What were the stewards' plans for ensuring continued supplies of raw materials and power? How would they be paid, and how would they purchase supplies? What would be done with the existing management, and how would charges of trespass be dealt with? But of all the questions, the most insistent was, what protection would workers have if they were injured during work organised by a workers' occupation, and by what means could they be insured?

The GEC stewards tried to secure answers to some of these technical problems from sympathetic trade union officers, but they were never able to present convincing blueprints for the solution of the majority of the questions. The most difficult questions were perhaps the easiest to answer: the workers would have been paid, if at all, out of solidarity funds, and they would almost certainly have been generously forthcoming. They would have been provisioned, if at all, as a result of solidarity action in other relevant plants and distribution services, which would have required the extension of active solidarity by trade unionists in other sectors of the economy. This would not have proved easy. Charges of trespass could only be brought if the use of force to remove the workers was contemplated by authority, so that litigation was not likely to be an immediate contingency, since such a battle, however it went, could only result in a great moral defeat for the authorities themselves. To the problem of insurance, there was no solid answer, at the time, even though several people thought they had found one.

In retrospect, the opinion of both the IWC and a number of GEC workers themselves was that in an industry such as that involved in Liverpool in which there were large-scale difficulties in securing both inputs of material and outlets to the market, 'working-in' was an unrealistic goal, and that the same result could have been achieved by a sit-in which announced its intention of working on once the problems of supplies and services had been solved, with the help of the trade unions. Such action would have called for an enormous effort by the Labour Movement, but it could well have succeeded.

But the GEC workforce was divided. The most intensively organised plant was at Netherton, and, apart from its aircraft section, this was scheduled for complete closure. Napiers, also well represented, was also marked down to be finished. But the least organised sector, the English Electric factory in the East Lancs Road, was only to share 300 dismissals among 8,000 employed there. Not unexpectedly, when the stewards' decision came to be reversed, it was some of the workers in this section who began the rebellion. They were stimulated by intensive hostile coverage in the newspapers, coupled with a 'personal' letter from the management which was also reproduced in the *Liverpool Echo*. Armed with a megaphone, they advanced on a platform at the mass meeting of September 17th, and successfully moved a resolution annulling the work-in. Only two days remained before the occupation was due, and these were filled with celebrations in the newspapers concerning the fundamental good sense and amenability of British workers, who were, it seems, not quite so bad after all.

Yet even the collapse of the Liverpool work-in was anything but a defeat, for it sowed ideas which were soon to grow and bear fruit. One of those who was profoundly influenced by the Liverpool events was Tony Benn. At the time he was Minister of Technology, and thus responsible for industry. He visited the plants on the day that the proposed occupation was to have taken place, and was intercepted and conducted around by the shop stewards' committee. He has subsequently commented upon the deep impression that this visit made on him, and it certainly influenced his attitudes to the predicament faced by the men of Clydeside two years later.

Why did the work-in work?

How, then, did the shop stewards at UCS succeed in establishing an occupation by the workpeople when Liverpool had previously failed? In 1969, national unemployment queues totalled more than 600,000 people, with some 30,000 of these on Merseyside. By 1971 more than 800,000 were out of work in Britain, almost 130,000 of whom were in Scotland. Both areas had a strongly militant tradition, and both had produced able leaders, so that neither of these conditions can explain the discrepancy between the two experiences. There was one major technical difference: at UCS the workers found themselves in control of an asset which became more valuable with each day of work – the ninety million pounds' worth of shipping under construction, which the pilots could always refuse to take down the Clyde until a satisfactory agreement was reached. There was also an important political difference: the Labour Government had fallen, and one of its most prominent and able spokesmen had become convinced that the Labour Party's future depended on its willingness to become the champion of the cause of industrial democracy.

It is perfectly clear, also, that leaders of the UCS initiative were well aware of the problems which had worried the Liverpool stewards before them. (They should have been: 2,000 copies of the IWC pamphlet recording the story of the GEC struggles were distributed in Glasgow between June 14th and July 30th.) Speaking at an IWC Conference in Newcastle-upon-Tyne,[6] Jimmy Airlie summed up the ideas of the Glasgow men in characteristically shrewd terms:

'It was not a simple matter, saying we would work-in: we realised that there would be certain problems, and one of the problems would be the questions that were raised before, during the planned GEC takeover, such as whether the workers could draw their redundancy pay, and what should be done about insurance and so on.

We attempted to answer these problems with our successes in the struggle. Of course, the government solved some of these problems when they set up their Committee of Enquiry, the 'Four Wise Men', who gave their report which in effect meant the butchery of the industry, slashing it from eight and a half thousand workers down to two and a half thousand, and demanding the acceptance of worse conditions, wages structures and so on. This Report really hardened the attitude of the workers. So the joint shop stewards' committee met and formulated the plan of the work-in, resulting in our taking over the gates and in effect saying we would control the yard. When we called a mass meeting of the workers, we got a unanimous decision to that effect. Then the questions which the joint shop stewards had to resolve were very complicated.'

First among these complex issues was the problem of what to do about redundancy:

'because many workers were liable to receive redundancy pay, and subsequently the liquidator did declare 800 workers redundant. So we had a debate: and it was that kind of sharp but constructive debate in which some of the lads were arguing, and understandably, that the men who were declared redundant should not accept redundancy pay because this would

94

be *de facto* acceptance of redundancy. But we argued that it would be quite wrong to look at things that way: that if the State wanted to pay a man around £800 that was its business: all that we were asking was that after he was paid his money he should still keep coming into the factory and we would alleviate his hardship.'

The next major topic to be resolved was that of insurance:

'Lads came forward to say, "What will happen if we get injured at work?" Our answer was: "Look brother, every day you go to work you're liable to get injured, so we're saying to you, don't get injured. But if you do, we'll give you this guarantee, that no one will suffer as a result of the work-in, or, if there is any suffering it will be on an equal basis, and because you're working-in you'll be working on the same conditions as if you were working out."'

Critics on the 'far' left have frequently claimed that UCS succeeded because it was a pseudo-action, not a 'real' one. Such criticisms should certainly be studied, but it must be said at the outset that they do not carry conviction. Once again, Jimmy Airlie provides a convincing reply.

'One of the main criticisms that we hear from certain quarters of the Labour Movement has been to the effect that the work-in has been "pseudo-revolutionary". Such critics say that we have been conning the workers, that we have set up something which is really only a big public relations job; and they tell us that we should sit-in, not work-in. In answer to all this, first of all, I would say that anybody who ever worked in a shipyard would not talk about sitting-in, but in any case we felt it would be wrong, tactically, and that ideologically it wasn't the right position.

I must stress that we have always said that we feel that the work-in applies to our particular position: we don't say that it will be the formula of every type of struggle. Sometimes, the sit-in is the best thing that can be done. The work-in suits some lads because of the nature of their particular industry. In other places it would not be a work-in or a sit-in: in the big multi-combines I would argue that with all the difficulties they've got with the combines, if there is a combine committee that operates effectively with a rank and file shop stewards committee, if you take over one factory you can at the same time appeal to all the other factories who'd all be stopping: that's the approach I would argue if I was working in a multi-combine factory. There's no one way to battle with redundancy. The only constant fact is that you struggle, because only through struggle can you develop the understanding of the workers.'

Whether or not the workers of West Central Scotland shared Jimmy Airlie's precise notions of the implications of these actions, the popular appeal which they made on their own merits was electric. The contrast, in the minds of these workers, was not how far the work-in fell short of some imaginary revolution, but how far it surpassed the previous overwhelmingly passive practice during arguments on redundancy. This, Airlie pointed out;

> 'Previously, in the West Central belt of Scotland, up and down this country, we have had bitter experiences of mass redundancies and closures, all of which have always been met with the timeworn formula that the MPs and the local full-time union officials would be called in to meet with the Employers' Association, who would then meet the representatives of the Department of Trade and Industry: but all the time the workers would be outside the gates waiting on their fates. The UCS work-in has been revolutionary in the sense that it has shown, here was a workforce which stood up to say "We have hopes, we have aspirations, and no one is going to negotiate above our heads: we're taking control of the yards and to move us you'll have to come in and get us!" I would suggest that whatever criticism may be made that event was revolutionary.'

Around UCS there was a threefold mobilisation of dramatic proportions.[7]

First, the Scottish trade unions rallied in two vast demonstrations which had enormous political meaning, and the Scottish TUC was drawn into a major campaign of action on behalf of UCS. Later, at the prompting of Tony Benn, this body successfully carried through the first social audit to be commissioned by British unions, which itself helped to create a rallying focus for the fight against unemployment.

Second, the Labour Movement from all over Britain was inspired to contribute enormous sums of money to maintain the work-in, and the initiative spread to other plants in different industries, including concerns which supplied the yards.

Third, the political institutions of Labour were drawn into the struggle, formally endorsing the UCS initiative and at the same time demanding a nationalised shipbuilding industry. Indeed, the Parliamentary Labour Party took up this cause even before the Party Conference, which is an unusual initiative for such a cautious body to make. None of this is in any way negligible.

These overall gains were undoubtedly affected by the very particular problems raised by the crisis on the Clyde, which, as a one-time strong point of the Scottish economy, became, in its decline, a symbol for all the more general difficulties of the Scots, arousing a very general national concern, which was reflected throughout the Scottish press, including some of the most conservative newspapers. (Not all, however. Some were disgracefully unfair.) Yet at the same time that UCS seemed to Scotland a dreadful warning of the likely prospects of other Scottish industries, it was also a most unpleasant omen for the rest of the shipbuilding industry throughout Britain. Extremely dependent on state contracts and direct aid, this declining sector was made more aware of its vulnerability by the apparent brutality of the government's decision to close the Upper Clyde. Such pressures ensured from the beginning that the UCS men would receive wide publicity, and this was brilliantly exploited by their rank-and-file leaders, notably by Jimmy Reid.

Yet, although such political gains have deep significance, the trade union scope of the work-in inevitably remained tied to the objective of rescuing as many jobs as possible within the available structure. The declared aim of the work-in at its commencement was to keep open all four shipyards comprising UCS and to maintain in employment the total labour force at the moment of liquidation, 8,500. In accordance with this aim, workers were advised to refuse to accept dismissal notices (although, as Jimmy Airlie pointed out, they were encouraged to accept payment of redundancy monies) and to remain at work under the authority of the shop stewards' co-ordinating committee, which supplemented the dispute benefit they were receiving from their unions by a weekly payment which equalled their previous half-year's average weekly earnings. About £9,000 a week was paid out throughout the work-in. The co-ordinating committee raised the wherewithal for these payments by its appeal for funds to the Labour Movement, which responded warmly. Support came not only from a cross-section of British trade union and radical organisations, but also from many foreign trade unions.

From inside the yards, each worker paid a levy of 50p a week to the fund. From outside, monies were sent by thousands of individuals. John Lennon sent a bunch of red roses and a large contribution:

collections were taken at meetings all over Britain, while donations came from as far away as Australia. (A crop of factory and mine occupations broke out in that country soon after the news of UCS was heard by Australian trade unionists.) Some forty stewards were elected to the co-ordinating committee, which sat continuously in daily meetings, and which heard regular reports from the convenors at the four yards, and from departmental stewards who held weekly meetings of the men in their sections. A finance committee was charged with a whole series of technical duties, such as paying the national insurance stamps of work-in 'employees', and with maintaining discretion about the exact state of the treasury for as long as was necessary to prevent the government from estimating the exact achievement of the work-in. £350,000 was paid out inside the yards in a period of some 40 weeks: at the same time, the UCS workers made generous contributions to appeals by other groups of workers as their initiative began to attract imitators. One estimate of the total fund raised puts it as £485,000[8] Another guesses 'at least half a million'.[9]

To maintain good communications, at intervals there were mass meetings in the four separate yards, and from time to time there were general meetings of all workers employed within the consortium.

The work of the yards was carefully regulated to ensure that the liquidator only received what he paid for, and this meant that workers who 'worked-in' were sometimes employed in maintaining the work-in itself. To avoid insurance problems, care was taken in the deployment of men who were 'working-in'. The most careful control was exercised over the deployment of capital equipment, and fully or partially finished ships could only be removed from their construction sites with the approval of the co-ordinating committee. At the same time, labour discipline was maintained by the committee, which drew up a series of rules, including the prohibition of drinking and fighting which was announced by Jimmy Reid at the commencement of the action. The difficulty inherent in the work-in was not, however, that such rules needed any elaborate enforcement. On the contrary, so great was the enthusiasm that a major problem became the restraint of production to pre-occupation levels. Obviously, the sooner that existing contracts were completed, the more immediate became the threat of further lay-offs. So the pace of work was restricted, in principle, to that which obtained before the June decision to close the yards.

Constant scrutiny by the media ensured that the workers' successes in overcoming the organisational difficulties which confronted them, many of which were the subject of prolonged public speculation, were borne home not only to other trade unionists, but also to the leading Labour politicians and the government itself. By the time of the Labour Conference in Autumn 1971, the UCS visiting delegation received an ecstatic welcome.

In February 1972 the government announced a grant of £35 million towards the reconstitution of three of the four yards, with a promise of additional aid to any prospective buyer of the fourth yard, Clydebank. The three yards, under the auspices of Govan Shipbuilders Ltd., became independently operational with a £35 million government contribution, on July 1st 1972: Marathon Manufacturing, a rigbuilding company, took over the fourth, with a £12 million grant, on October 10th when the work-in was ended. Altogether the government was to pay out more than £47 million.

First published in 1981

Footnotes
1. *The Scotsman,* 15th June 1971.
2. Alasdair Buchan: *The Right to Work – The Story of the Upper Clyde Confrontation,* Calder and Boyars, 1972, p.14.
3. Cf. Jack McGill: *Crisis on the Clyde,* Davis-Poynter, 1973.
4. Ken Fleet: an unpublished brief for the UCS social audit, organised by the STUC.
5. Cf. *GEC-EE Workers' Takeover,* IWC Pamphlet No.17, 1969.
6. Held at Henderson Hall, Newcastle University, on January 8th-9th 1972.
7. For an account of these responses, see Jack McGill: *Crisis on the Clyde,* Davis-Poynter, 1973, Chapters II et seq. Also W. Thompson and Finlay Hart: *The UCS Work-In,* Lawrence and Wishart, 1972.
8. Terry Bishop, When the Workers Take Control, *Personnel Management,* journal of the Institute of Personnel Management: March 1973.
9. North East TU Studies Unit, *Workers' Occupations and the North-East Experience,* 1976, p.20.

6
Industrial Democracy
and the Quality of Life

In the years following 1968, a growing procession of European trade unionists began to be seen at IWC Conferences. They included, from Italy, Pino Tagliazucchi and Bruno Trentin; from France, Serge Mallet and Michel Rocard, later to become a leader of the French Socialist Party and Prime Minister; and representatives from the oppositional forces in Spain and Portugal, still at the time living under dictatorship.

An important breakthrough in 1972 came with the special conference organised by the German Metalworkers' Union, IG Metall. This took place in Oberhausen from the 11th – 14th April, and brought together political leaders from all over Europe, including Erhard Eppler, Olof Palme, Tony Benn, Pierre Naville, Adam Schaff and Walter Arendt, the Federal Minister of Labour in Bonn. Numerous scholars participated, alongside trade union representatives.

This is an excerpt from my paper, which was based on a book which I wrote jointly with Tony Topham, and which was later published, in 1974, by Penguin Books, under the title The New Unionism.

Arguments about the quality of life in industrial society have recently taken on an urgency and stridency which, if belated, is none the less welcome to all who have a lingering fondness for mankind. As our air is poisoned, our rivers and seas made sterile, or worse, virulent with hostile elements, our countryside desecrated and our very future as a species put in doubt by the profligate consumption of such all too finite resources as remain available to us, so, somewhat after the eleventh hour, we begin to complain. It is right to try to save the environment. Yet the one virtually infinite resource which mankind possesses is that of *human* potential which is most stupidly, and most cruelly, thwarted by the present rapacious economic order, at whose door most other complaints against pollution of both nature and society must also be laid.

The founder of cybernetics, Norbert Wiener, was keenly aware of the waste of human capacity involved in modern industry.

'In my mind' he wrote 'use of a human being in which less is demanded of him than his full stature is a degradation and a waste. It is a degradation to a human being to chain him to an oar and use him as a source of power, but it is an almost equal degradation to assign him to a purely repetitive task in a factory, which demands less than a millionth of his brain capacity. It is simpler to organise a factory or a galley which uses human beings for a trivial fraction of their worth than it is to provide a world in which they can grow to their full stature.'[1]

But the 'full stature' of a human being is a developing stature, in which intellect, passion and will are all free to assert themselves. Wiener's cry of pain for the people who are mutilated in our society is in no way novel, and has antecedents in moral philosophy which date back at least as far as the thought of Immanuel Kant.

The dictum of Kant 'always treat humanity in your own person and in others as an end and never as a means', merely holds out a criterion for human behaviour which, while it retains its appeal, is quite clearly inoperable in our society. All economic activity, all productive organisation in capitalist industry is based upon the systematic violation of the categorical imperative. In every factory, mine, office and government department we find that men and women are compelled to labour to realise goals which have been determined by others, to augment the power and prestige of others, to enrich others and enlarge their influence and status. Employees are not merely subordinates: they find their subordination intensified by the fact that their interests and aspirations can be imposed or manipulated by social forces quite beyond their individual or collective control. Most workplaces do not even leave their workpeople free to fix even their own speed or rhythm of toil, while often even their pauses and rest-breaks, postures and work-dispositions are externally, and all too arbitrarily, determined. Legions of workers are driven deaf by noise-levels which are insupportable by normal human beings, or have their sight impaired, or suffer physical mutilation by the inexorable side-effects of industrial processes. It is impossible for those who administer this state of affairs to claim that the maxim 'do as you would be done by' is even remotely applicable to their conduct.

101

Yet the opponents of this state of affairs are in no stronger position to act upon the Kantian prescription than those against whom they react. Trade unions and political parties, if they operate within the established structures, must strike a daily progression of compromises with those forces which are based upon the use of men as objects, as tools in some greater purpose of capital aggrandisement. Even those who reject the given system completely, and opt for its revolutionary overthrow, can have no immediate use for Kant. They require to establish counter-institutions, an alternative division of political and military labour, in which it is quite impossible to treat every man as 'an end in himself'. This fact was recognised by Trotsky, who wrote:

> 'A means can only be justified by its end. But the end in turn needs to be justified... and the end is justified if it leads to increasing the power of man over nature and to the abolition of the power of man over man.'[2]

The English sociologist Ginsberg[3] saw this notion as purely Kantian in its scope. However, there are good grounds for judging it to be quite different from Kant's injunction: it is applicable to our present problems, while Kant's is not. By introducing a distinct component of relativism, and by transferring its prescription from the present (as edict) to the future (as ultimate aim), Trotsky sets out a line of march, rather than an initial commandment. But such a line of march can be pursued in different formations, at different speeds, and with means by no means uniform with those Trotsky felt to be imperative. The struggle to overcome the power of one man over another will certainly recur in capitalist industry: it has by no means exhausted its impulse, and to think that it could cease would be to imagine that humanity was capable of choosing helotry at a time when its technical capacity for freedom had never been greater. What is clear, however, is that struggle will take experimental forms, as it has throughout the whole history of the Labour Movement:[4] that it will essay a whole variety of initiatives, learning all the time that it acts.

In this sense, the movement for workers' control of industry is profoundly revolutionary, even while it pursues the most limited reforms. At the same time, if any socialist movement represents the continuation, development and realisation of the basic liberal criteria of democracy, it is this one, because it is impossible to agitate for the growth of democratic forms complex enough to govern the enormous scope of modern industry without comprehending every significant lesson which has been learnt in the parallel, but simpler, struggle to impose accountability upon the governors of political institutions.

Quite clearly, it is absurd to speak of real democracy, of real accountability, in institutions which are dominated by property. In today's industry, a handful of owners not merely command obedience from a vast mass of employees, but have so arranged affairs that the most active productive efforts of their subordinates can only intensify their dependence.[5] The greater their productivity, the greater the augmentation of hostile powers which may be used against them, even to the point of their own displacement from labour itself. The reality of this process has been made abundantly plain in Britain, where in recent years, between 1963 and 1971, indices of employment have moved from 100 down to 94.5, while those of productivity have moved from 100 up to 117. Not to put too fine a point on matters, the associated labours of workpeople in Britain have thus produced an alien power which has precipitated something like one million of their brethren out of work altogether.[6] Unfortunately, this story repeats itself in other countries wherever the same conditions apply. Even when operating at its most efficient optimum levels, capital can only intensify the subordination and degradation against which Wiener was raging. The signs today seem to be that this optimum, with its concomitant 'affluence', is in increasingly acute peril. No doubt this partly explains the renewed interest in socialism and in industrial democracy.

Advocates of industrial democracy fall into two species. There are those who either wish to embellish a fundamentally undemocratic structure with decorous descriptions, or who are gulled into accepting such pretences for reality. And there are those who wish to socialise private property in productive organisations, and to extend to industry the same presumptions which are alleged to govern political institutions in the most advanced capitalist democracies. The first category speaks a great deal about 'workers' participation in industry' without ever impinging on the hard realities which impel workers *not* to participate. Their strategems were summarised in the wall-poster which appeared in Paris during the 1968 upsurge:

I participate
Thou participatest
He participates
We participate
You participate
They profit

The second category do not usually speak about 'participation', although when they do, they mean something more than subordinate consultation. They usually speak of 'workers' control' as their prescription for the erosion of arbitrary power in plant, industry and economy in capitalist society, and of 'workers' self-management' as their goal for a socialist society.[7]

Of course, this terminology is by no means universally accepted, so there remain possibilities for semantic disputes. On one side, workpeople are apt to take the promises of 'participation' or 'consultation' seriously, so that frequently demands which might legitimately be characterised as claims for more control are made under the formulae of insistence upon 'fuller participation' or 'proper consultation'.[8] At another extreme, some socialists use the term 'workers' control' to describe their norms for the administration of socialised economies, and simultaneously decry the more conventional trade union demand which organises itself around the same slogan, as at best a palliative, at worst a delusion.[9] Yet there is very considerable evidence that various controls *can*, within limits, be encroached from the unilateral disposition of management by alert trade unions in certain favourable conditions. Of course, all free collective bargaining denies unilateral managerial control over wages, hours, and certain types of working conditions. But in every advanced Western European country some trade unions have gone far beyond imposing such elementary restrictions, to establish varying degrees of control over hiring, firing, training, speeds and dispositions of work, health, safety regulations and their enforcement, and in some cases, over access to accounts and apposite financial information concerning the prospects of the firm.[10] In many cases, legal powers for limited controls may be secured by trade union political pressure, as in the notable instance of the legally established workmen's inspectorate in the British coal-mining industry. It should be stressed, however, that all attempts in Britain to extend similar powers to workers in manufacturing industry, or even to employees in the notoriously dangerous deep-sea fishing fleets and the merchant navy, have so far proved fruitless.

In the words of Hugh Scanlon, President of the British engineers' union, the AUEW;

'There already exists, particularly in fully unionised concerns, a considerable degree of workers' control in individual factories, if "workers' control" is defined as effective control by organised workers over the arbitrary powers of management. This is indeed "the seed of the new society inside the old". Shop stewards prefer, and seem to get more out of, workshop bargaining than the type of "consultation" favoured by management. This radical move away from the defensive mentality of the past is graphically shown in the fact concerning the causes of industrial disputes. It has been shown that between 1940 and 1960, the proportion of strikes (excluding strikes in the mining industry) not directly concerned with wage-increases, but connected with disputes such as those about working arrangements, rules and discipline, have risen from about one-third to three-quarters of the total. In 1960, a TUC survey showed that only 32% of strikes were directly about money: 29% were about dismissals alone. In this brief survey it is clear that the changes in the Labour Movement since the thirties are making nonsense of the concept of a purely 'economic man', limited to actions in defence of his standard of living. Far wider issues are involved today.

Yet even the extension of the current type of 'workers' control' can be seen as holding only a watching and limiting function on the 'rights' of management. Workers are demanding an *effective* voice in management policy. This aspiration is particularly concentrated in regard to the nationalised industries,where obviously the greatest scope is offered to the demand that management be obliged to obtain the consent of workers in all matters of industrial policy. Trade unions envisage a radical extension of the scope of collective trade union action, from a point beyond wages and salaries to human conditions of employment in their broadest aspects.'[11]

Similar views have been expressed by many British trade union leaders, notably Jack Jones,[12] the General Secretary of the largest union in Britain, the Transport and General Workers' Union; Ernie Roberts, the Engineer's Assistant Secretary; Alan Fisher, the Public Employees' leader, and spokesmen of the Post Office and Technicians' unions.[13] Demands along the same lines are particularly evident in the agendas of some of the most dynamic white-collar unions, where physical proximity to managerial personnel and close familiarity with some of the crucial problems involved in decision-taking clearly have no noticeable effect in damping the appetite of employees for a non-servile status.

This current of thought is by no means confined to British labour. Perhaps the most coherent statement of trade union aspirations for industrial democracy, and the most integrally thought-out strategy to achieve such aims is to be found in the programme which was adopted in 1971 by the Belgian Socialist Unions, organised in the General Federation of Belgian Workers (see Chapter 8).

First published in 1972

Footnotes

1. Norbert Wiener, *The Human Use of Human Beings*, Boston, 1950, p.16.
2. Leon Trotsky, *Their Morals and Ours*, Pioneer Books, New York, 1968.
3. Morris Ginsberg, *Evolution and Progress*, Heinemann, London, 1961, pp.252-3.
4. We have documented some of the wide variety of these forms as exemplified in the recent history of the British Labour Movement, in K. Coates & A. Topham, *Industrial Democracy in Great Britain*, MacGibbon & Kee, London, 1968 (subsequently issued in a paperback edition by Panther books of London and then in four volumes by Spokesman Books).
5. For a discussion of the English evidence on this matter, see Michael Barratt Brown: *The Controllers of British industry*, in *Can the Workers Run industry?* ed. K. Coates, Institute for Workers' Control, Nottingham, 1968. Also Robin Murray two articles in *The Spokesman*, Nos. 10 and 11, 'The International Company' and 'The State and the Internationalisation of Capital'.
6. John Hughes: *Behind the Dole Queue, The Facts about Unemployment*, Spokesman pamphlet No. 23, 1971.
7. For an extended discussion of these problems, see my *Essays on Industrial Democracy*, Spokesman Books, 1971.
8. As has been explained by Ernie Roberts in *Workers' Control and the Trade Unions*, published in *Can The Workers Run Industry?* loc. cit.
9. The 'palliative' view has been expressed by some leading British communists, and can be found discussed in *The Debate on Workers' Control* published by IWC, Nottingham, 1970. The 'delusion' view has been strenuously argued by certain Marxist-Leninist (Maoist) leaders in Britain, notably Mr. Reg Birch, in the journal *The Worker*, October, 1970.
10. Some of the evidence on these matters is to be found in the study by Coates and Topham: *The New Unionism*, Peter Owen, London, 1972, Penguin Books, 1974.

11. Cf. Hugh Scanlon: *The Way Forward for Workers' Control,* IWC, Nottingham, 1971.
12. Cf. Jones' contribution to the Labour Party debate on industrial democracy, in Coates, Barratt Brown and Topham, *The Trade Union Register,* Merlin Press, London, 1969.
13. The British postmen have long preached a doctrine of workers' control, and have in fact published a number of pamphlets on the question ever since the heyday of Guild Socialism in the immediate post-war years after 1918. The re-organisation of the Post Office under the Wilson administration brought about an exchange of recriminating polemics between the responsible minister and the Union of Post Office Workers, on precisely these questions. Cf. *Bulletin of the Institute for Workers' Control,* Vol. 1, 1968.

7

Education as a Lifelong Experience

'Education as a lifelong experience' was written as a contribution to an anthology prepared by Peter Buckman, and published by the Souvenir Press in 1973. This, Education Without Schools, was provoked by the essay of Ivan Illich, 'De-schooling Society'. This was an argument for a new environment in which growing up could be classless, 'or we will get a brave new world in which Big Brother educates us all'.

What is the relationship between education and industry? This is a crucial question, but it is quite commonly avoided by educationalists, and particularly by educational reformers. Whenever we do meet it, it is usually to find that those asking it have subtly transformed it in order to assume an answer which is not too discomfiting either to the teaching profession or to industrialists. Of course, the question 'what does industry need from education?' poses quite a different set of problems to those we need to discuss. 'How can education better serve industry?' is the sort of conundrum that arises with every new phase of technological development: more schools, more colleges and universities must be opened to provide more scientists, more administrators, and more technically qualified workpeople, we are told at intervals of about a generation. The priorities in such questions are upside down and back to front. To see things the right way up, and to begin the pursuit of *education,* we must ask 'what sort of factories do our schools need?'

In the abstract, taking formal schooling at its best, there are few teachers who will not, when pushed, lay claim to the fundamental liberal commitment that their role is to stimulate the fullest possible development of their charges. The school, they feel, is properly an incubator of the free personality. That is to say, teachers commonly assume, or to be more accurate, think they assume, that they should treat their students each as an end in himself, and never as a mere means to serve some greater goal: whether that goal be the imagined good of the State, or the anticipated productivity of the Economy, or even, in these agnostic days, the alleged purpose of the Almighty. The old Jesuit boast that given care of a child until he reached the age of seven, he would be kept forever in the faith, is seen by the dominant educational consensus of today as almost the very epitome of evil. True, there are some who would explicitly repudiate liberal pretensions, but there are numerous good liberal swearwords to describe the results of such apostasy. 'Indoctrination', 'manipulation', 'brain-washing', 'propagandising' all spring to mind.

To remain on an equally abstract plane, there is not a factory, an office, a mine or a depot in the land in which these basic liberal assumptions can hold sway for a fraction of a moment, not even on Christmas Day when everyone is on holiday. No employer can treat his employees as ends in themselves, whose free personal de-velopment is the prime object of his enterprise. Indeed, no employer, however powerful, can easily imagine being so treated himself, even though it is his will, or the will of the élite grouping of which he forms a part, which has determined, often in precise detail, the major life options which are open to, or closed from, his subordinates. Few employers today actually *tell* their workmen that they are paid to work, not to think: but none are able to predicate their activities on any assumption other than that the goals and strategies of the enterprise, insofar as they are determined by anyone at all, must be rigidly monopolised by its directorate. Throughout the majority of modern industry, it is fair to be far more precise than this: individual initiative by an employee is commonly seen as at best an embarrassment, at worst a disruption, while the personal development of employees is considered a matter for their own pursuit, as best they can arrange it, in those parts of their lives which are called 'leisure'. Industry still seeks square pegs for square holes, and round pegs for round holes. Even in the comparatively rare cases where jobs are 'enlarged', or rotated, the modern division of labour remains, for the overwhelming majority of people, an absolute barrier to the development of their productive, or creative, capacities in any field other than the narrow strip to which they have been allotted. Proficiencies which can be learnt in days or weeks frequently become life-expectations. Such horizons can only tend to reduce people, unless they find ways to rebel against them.

The brutalising of work tends to turn leisure into passivity, or into an aggressively private activity: the alienated antithesis of compulsory labour. Modern industry, modern capitalism, far from constituting a celebration of the freedom of the individual, in fact represents a most systematic and extended denial of the basic conditions of that freedom.

But these are abstract statements, statements moreover of tendency, and they represent only part of the truth. The complex reality is that conditions of unfreedom repeatedly stimulate moods of rejection. Good schools reinforce this rejection, which will only hold out new hopes of fulfilment when subjection no longer remains the rule.

It remains true that the liberal educational goals are, at root, in flagrant contradiction to the basic assumptions which regulate our economic life. The result is that today, far from education – individual development in co-operative activity – reaching out through working life to become a life-long experience, it is still true that industry constantly exerts itself to reach its clammy hands down into the schools, in order to make wage-slavery as lifelong, and as inescapable, as it possibly can. Of course, there are gross difficulties in the process. Although it is true that there are still all too many infant schools in which five-year-olds are aligned in ranks in wet play-grounds and whistled into assembly, a ritual which is only meaningful as house-training for the factory and the clocking-in queue, yet it remains quite undeniable that modern pedagogy (which is the more necessary to industry as it desperately roots round to find expanded off-square pegs to fit the new precision-made eccentric holes of modern technology) is persistently rolling back the age at which authoritarian discipline can be introduced. Opening the 1972 Conference of the British National Union of Teachers, the President of the organisation claimed that in recent years there had been 'a new spirit in the schools. The primary school today' he said, 'is a place of adventure, experiment, liveliness, joy, and a felicitous co-operation between child, parent and teacher.'

Such progress notwithstanding, and there is still room for a great deal more of it, the school still serves its masters. The more co-operative and participatory that teaching techniques become, the more grossly they will be out of phase with the roles for which their victims are being prepared. The raising of the school leaving age may see a rise in the age of secondary school mutiny: but mutiny remains as likely as ever to nullify even the best pedagogic intentions as the transition from classroom to workshop becomes imminent. In the best imaginable case, if the schools were to succeed in wholly dedicating themselves to the stimulation and liberation of imagination throughout the whole school-life of their pupils, then those pupils would be powerfully tempted to drop out of the society into which they were subsequently evicted. There are reformers, like Paul Goodman, who welcome this prospect. To me it seems an unlikely blessing. Denied access to any satisfactory outlet for productive effort, and denied facilities for creative communication unless they show exceptional talents, such rebels are likely to develop into shallow hedonists, whose lives will be prone to sterile introversion and dependency. If hedonism is a life-style, it is scarcely a *human* life-style: evolution could well have been arrested with the emergence of the common cat, or for all we know, the garden slug, leaving ample possibilities for self-satisfaction at this sad level of expectation. If it were possible for schools to ignore industry during the whole period of compulsory education, and it is not, it would still be ethically impermissible for them to tolerate a factory system which would give their pupils the choice of forgetting the most important things they had learnt, or lapsing into social parasitism. In fact, up to now, this discussion implies, if anything, far too rosy a picture of the state of school autonomy from the industrial power-complex. The whole system of public examinations has no imaginable educational function, but is indispensable to the Labour Exchange. Tests of certain kinds can help both teachers and students: but they help best when the student understands that perhaps their most crucial function is to help the teacher overcome his own inadequacies. There never was a mark awarded that said anything incontrovertible about the ability of a student, because 'ability' is a term which includes a vast area of potential which can never be measured until after it has been realised, and which can (and should) remain open throughout a lifetime: but every mark ever given does say something quite final about the level

111

of actual communication that has taken place between a teacher and his charge. 'Bring out number, weight and measure' said Blake 'in a year of dearth'. The mania for evaluation of students' performance would be a healthy event, if it were a self-critical pedagogic device. As it is, it tends to present a recurrent libel on the capacities of those 'evaluated', which has the effect, all too often, of self-fulfilling prophecy, convincing its victims that *they* suffer from incapacities which are not in truth their own, but their institutions'. Of course, if an employer wants a French-speaking secretary, he has to know that she can in fact speak French before he can employ her. Exams will be with us for a while yet: but we should know for what they were spawned, and refuse them the dignity of an *educational* rationale. Yet, in a negative way, they show us what vast developments are possible, by revealing some fraction of the *needs* which our current school system can never begin to meet. It is precisely when we are confronted by the results of measurements of 'performance' that we become aware of the pervasive influence of social status on the school structure. Poor kids do badly, rich kids do well. As J. W. B. Douglas reports in *The Home and the School:*

> 'When housing conditions are unsatisfactory, children make relatively low scores in the tests. This is so in each social class, but whereas middle-class children, as they get older, reduce this handicap, the manual working-class children from unsatisfactory homes fall even further behind; for them, overcrowding and other deficiencies at home have a progressive and depressive influence on their test performance.'

Bad housing is important as an indicator of this phenomenon, but its real root is occupational. Unskilled workers are badly paid, which is why they live on poor estates or in slums. Slum housing is certainly a handicap, but it is not an insuperable handicap on its own. Half-blind Sean O'Casey saw more colour in the world from a Dublin tenement than most duchesses can find in a room full of Titians. Abraham Lincoln was reportedly conceived in a log cabin, but his step-mother taught him to read the Bible, *Pilgrim's Progress,* and *Robinson Crusoe.* You have to apply other clamps to the imagination than poor housing if you are to achieve any success in the effort to paralyse it. In British slums, the majority of fathers and mothers have never been introduced to Bunyan or Defoe, or for that matter to any other major writer in our language, so it is hardly surprising if their children read late, and with difficulty. For years it was fashionable to consider this fact as the outcome of genetic determination. The unskilled were not culturally deprived because they were poor and unskilled, but because they were born that way. This was not the view of the classic theorists of industrialism. Adam Smith, who began his greatest work with the celebration of the productive merits of the division of labour, was well aware of its baneful influence on the labourer. His insights on this matter were enlarged in different ways by Owen, Ruskin, and Marx, to say nothing of the whole Pleiad of romantic novelists, poets, and publicists. What is perfectly clear is that as factories stabilised themselves as the predominant form of productive unit through society, so the divergence of talents was widened, and transmitted across generations. The industrial division of labour became the solid foundation of an industrial class system. For all its onesidedness, there are few descriptions of this process which are more compelling and more farsighted than that of de Tocqueville, in *Democracy in America:*

'When a workman is unceasingly and exclusively engaged in the fabrication of one thing, he ultimately does his work with singular dexterity; but at the same time he loses the general faculty of applying his mind to the direction of the work. He every day becomes more adroit and less industrious; so that it may be said of him that in proportion as the workman is improved the man is degraded... When a workman has spent a considerable portion of his existence in this manner, his thoughts are for ever set upon the object of his daily toil; his body has contracted certain fixed habits, which it can never shake off: in a word, he no longer belongs to himself, but to the calling which he has chosen. It is in vain that laws and manners have been at pains to level all barriers around such a man, and to open to him on every side a thousand different paths to fortune: a theory of manufactures more powerful than manners and laws binds him to a craft, and frequently to a spot, which he cannot leave: it assigns him a certain place in society beyond which he cannot go: in the midst of universal movement it has rendered him stationary.

In proportion as the principle of the division of labour is more extensively applied, the workman becomes more weak, more narrow-minded, and more dependent. The art advances, the artisan recedes...'

This savage prophecy has not been by any means fulfilled in full, for two good reasons. First, for the reason that people *will* resist dehumanisation, however high the cost of resistance, and however long the odds against their success. The whole story of trade unionism, and the entire vicarious history of the socialist movement, bear witness to this fact. As a result of it, the basic liberal humanist ideals survive the process which de Tocqueville traced, which is, of course, at one level, itself the result of the operation of the liberal doctrine in economic life. Secondly, the prophecy fails because the story of the development of industrial capitalism is an account of the unleashing of a succession of technological upheavals, during which the division of labour is recurrently recast. On one side this results from time to time in the demand for new skills and higher educational levels: but at the same time, on the other side it repeatedly gives rise to the displacement of old skills and the social rejection of all those people whose inflexibility (whether because they are old, or because they have been inadequately taught in their youth) keeps them below the threshold of profitable employment. So-called technological unemployment is not a new phenomenon, although in its recent forms it has the capacity to create wider unease in the body politic than heretofore. Its true source is not abstract technology, which, being inanimate, is socially neutral, but specific technologies in the service of capital, whose dominance depends upon the control of equipment and processes, and upon the subordination of the interests of people to the imperatives of its balance-sheets.

Adam Smith had adumbrated three component benefits of the division of labour: it augmented productivity by specialisation, increasing the proficiency of workmen by intensifying their dexterity; it saved time by cutting out transfers between operations; and it facilitated the introduction and development of machines. To these three principles, Charles Babbage, in *The Economy of Manufactures,* added a fourth:

> 'That the master manufacturer, by dividing the work to be executed into different processes, each requiring different degrees of skill and force, can purchase exactly that precise quantity of both of which is necessary for each process.'

114

With this perception rose the possibility of the whole school of scientific management, as subsequently developed by F. W. Taylor in the United States. The more intensively processes could be controlled, the more dependent roles were created for employees, and the less the industrial currency of the liberal ideal of an integrated human personality. Babbage recorded the process in 1832 without noticing the implication of his words:

> '...if the whole work were to be executed by one workman, that person must possess sufficient skill to perform the most difficult, and sufficient strength to execute the most laborious, of the operations into which the art is divided.'

Just about fifty years were to elapse before Taylor was to refine this insight to the point where he could insist, without shame, that:

> 'One of the very first requirements for a man who is fit to handle pig iron as a regular occupation is that he shall be so stupid and so phlegmatic that he more nearly resembles an ox than any other type.'

The logical result of such specialisation was clearly expressed in the dire anti-utopia of H. G. Wells' *The Time Machine,* in which exploration of the future revealed that effete aristocrats and feelingless plebians had evolved into two distinct and incompatible species. If the logical result is not to be anticipated in the actual outcome, we owe the fact both to human resilience and to the contradictory implications of advancing techniques. While Taylorism in its classic prescriptions gained a considerable following, in spite of protests, in the mass production industries of the Ford school, subsequent work methods have evolved alongside electronic techniques to produce quite different notions of job control. Nevertheless, Taylorism was an innovatory discipline which cast a long shadow before it, and even today, in the discussion of job-enlargement, rotation of tasks, 'participatory' reform, and kindred expedients, the ghost of scientific management can still be heard speaking, in a variety of accents it is true, but with no diminution of its anti-human intent. It is the same ghost which speaks in the debate on educational methods and reform of the schools. 'More means worse', it says. Selection and specialisation are its necessary watchwords. Its cardinal principle it transfers from Babbage's factories to the secondary modern schools and the lower streams of the alleged comprehensives which spring up on all sides. 'Spend no more than is necessary on human formation' it whispers. Surplus of training is dysfunctional: overeducated operatives are indisciplined and refractory. In a square hole, square people are optimal, and tendencies to deviate into roundness must be rigidly clamped out.

Yet all the time, industry needs education. A modest explosion has recently taken place in certain forms of continuation courses, in adult classes of a particular kind, in shop steward training, and in technical education, since the passage in Britain of the Industrial Training Act, which levies a toll on firms in order to ensure that if they do not train their own workers, they will be forced to pay to train other people's. A much bigger convulsion is called for, but is unlikely to take place. But all this effort, and most of the proposed effort which will not be undertaken, is conceived within the essential framework of the constricting assumptions we have been discussing. We *could* have a real transformation in education *at* work, but the price would not be simply the universalisation of day-release courses, desirable though that may be. A genuine transformation would involve education *in* work, self-education, community education, in the generation of real moves towards collective self-management of industry. Only such a revolution would abolish the stultifying role-patterns which are imposed on work-people, and only such a revolution would open up the possibility, and the need, for every man to seek the continuous enlargement of his powers and his basic knowledge of the world in which he was working.

Universalist education is incompatible with the rigid division of labour which forms men into porters and philosophers, and aligns them into opposing social classes. Both in work, and in whatever preparation which enlightened people come to agree it may be necessary to make for work, the division of labour as we understand it is more than a net disincentive to free personal development. Within it, 'equality of opportunity' comes to mean the will-o'-the-wisp of an equal start in a fundamentally unequal race: and all the nobility of the watch-word is transformed into sleazy apologetics. Free development of each personality to its outer limits means the systematic encouragement and fostering of talents, and this will never begin until factories begin to be schools, and self-governing schools at that. Only then will schools cease to be factories for the engineering of human beings into employees. Perhaps a hundred years ago, this was a utopian message. Today, it is direly practical: the only resource which we possess in virtual abundance is that of human potential, and yet it is that resource which we squander with even greater profligacy than we eat up the earth's finite material resources. Mankind will soon need all the wits and creativity which it is stifling every day in modern industry, and its appendage, modern education, if it is to find the way to live out another century.

First published in 1973

8

A Lesson from Belgium

The dialogue with European trade unionists continued. A joint seminar was organised between the IWC, the Belgian FGTB, or Socialist Trade Union Federation, and the French CFDT, which had begun life as a Christian Trade Union Centre, taking on an increasingly radical colouring. All three organisations were profoundly concerned to extend industrial democracy, but the dialogue was not simple or plain sailing, because each trade union centre had different traditions, and operated in different industrial relations systems. In spite of great goodwill it was not easy to find a common language. The French were committed to a policy of autogestion, or self-management, and saw the Belgian commitment to workers' control as being, to some degree, a compromised and irresolute position.

For the most part, IWC members did not see the two objectives as contradictory. In any case, the programme of the Belgian trade unions was sufficiently detailed, and sufficiently close to the thinking of IWC trade unionists in Britain, to constitute a strong encouragement. We published a translation of the programme in 1971, under the title A Trade Union Strategy in the Common Market. *This was the introduction to that book.*

The Belgian trade unions, which organise almost two million members, are among the strongest, proportionally speaking, in Europe and constitute a major social force in their own country. 66.95% of the eligible workpeople in Belgium are enrolled in their unions: the result is that these organisations are able to play a major part in the political life of the country, and between them sustain well over 100 members of Parliament. The short-run political influence of the trade union movement is, rather strangely, actually increased by the fact that two major federations exist: one aligned with the Socialist Party, and the other with the Catholic Christian Social Party. What must certainly constitute a source of weakness in many struggles has at the same time the paradoxical effect of exposing the Catholic Party to internal pressure from its allied trade unions, a pressure from which it cannot escape in the same way as it most certainly would, if all unions were affiliated to the rival Socialist Party.[1] Doubtless, this fact plays its own part in incorporating Belgian workers into the political structures which they have inherited: but for this, authority must pay a certain price in sensitivity to the corporate interests of Labour.

In 1965, membership of the various central union federations was as follows:

Confederation of Christian Unions (CSC)	844,430
Belgian General Federation of Labour (FGTB)	734,805
General Central Association of Liberal Trade Unions (CGSLB)	122,299
Central Association of Unified Unions	42,500
Independent Unions' Centre	58,000
Total	1,802,034

The two major federations are associated with the major political[2] parties. Most of the 'Liberal' unionists (for which in current English terms, 'conservative' might be a better rubric) are recruited from professional strata. The reasons for the numerical preponderance of the Catholic Unions have more to do with the development of the Belgian economy than with any primarily ideological commitment: each union centre has always drawn its main strength from certain areas of the country, and the power base of the Socialist FGTB has been in the declining French-speaking Walloon provinces, hard hit by the retrenchments in the coal and steel industries; while the growth sector of the economy has been in the predominantly Catholic Flemish-speaking coastal provinces, in which three-quarters of the members of the CSC are to be found. But Christian trade unionism has not come to the front in Belgium by means of simple inertia and sectarian commitment: it has in fact benefited from the rise of new social attitudes in the Church, and it has attracted a substantial cadre of active and capable organisers. The greater membership of the CSC is more dispersed than that of the FGTB, which is concentrated into a number of large-scale industries. Twelve industrial centres are affiliated to the FGTB: fourteen to the CSC. The Catholic unions recruit widely in textiles, food, and chemicals. In the FGTB, the three

119

major organisations of engineering workers, public service employees, and general workers account between them for 67% of the total membership.[3]

The background to the development of industry in Belgium cannot be understood without understanding the strange game of leapfrog which has gone on between Wallonia and Flanders since the constitution of the Belgian national state.

The first industrial revolution was, in Belgium, concentrated in Wallonia. From the second half of the eighteenth century, wool, coal, linen and cotton industries began to develop in the modern sense. Individual entrepreneurs gave place to joint-stock companies between 1825 and 1835, under the stimulus of the first major bank in the country, *La Société Générale*. As Ernest Mandel has pointed out, this was

'From the beginning a mixed bank, that is both a deposit and an investment bank, owning important holdings in innumerable industrial, financial, commercial and transport concerns. Belgium is thus the birthplace of finance capital in the Marxist sense: banking capital which flows into industry, substitutes shares for credit, and exercises close control over company management. Belgian finance capital acquired a dominant position in the economy of the country half a century before the same phenomenon occurred in Germany, France, U.S.A., Italy and elsewhere.'[4]

As Mandel comments, it is not at all surprising that Belgium became, in turn, the first mainland European country to start building railways; the owner of the densest rail-network in the world; the pioneer of railway-building abroad as far afield as Russia, Egypt, Mexico and China; a prodigious exporter of capital and techniques, and the proprietor of a Royal Colony, the Congo, administered by the *Société Générale*. Up to 1914 the opulence of the Belgian middle-classes was unrivalled, as was the squalor of the workers. The Catholic culture was reinforced by the fact that the Church dominion over education was only breached with difficulty during a protracted struggle with the Liberal Party: throughout this struggle the political structure was jealously controlled by the upper and middle classes, organised into Catholic and Liberal Parties. The working-class battle for the suffrage was particularly long drawn-out and hard. After a General Strike in 1893 the right to vote was gained by male workers, but this operated within the framework of a plural voting system, which seriously handicapped the working-class electors. The Catholic Party began to form its trade unions only when the battle for equal male suffrage was about to be conceded, as it was, in the end, after the First World War. But once the decision had been taken, the Catholic Church put out a formidable range of co-operative and social organisations which, linked with the new unions, and concentrated in the still largely rural provinces, provided for new industrialists a much needed alternative to the militant socialist unions which had come to dominate the already industrialised French-speaking provinces. The enhanced stability of labour relations in Flanders brought in its turn further industrial development.

Mandel has documented the close interplay between class and region in Belgian political life. In a nutshell, Flanders remained not only economically, but also politically subordinate until the early thirties. A national resurgence of Flemings, part-socialist, part-fascist, supported by some of the lesser clergy, but opposed by the Catholic hierarchy (as in the national struggle in Ireland) finally gained equal linguistic rights in 1932. From this time onwards, the majority party in Belgium was 'naturally' Catholic and, indeed, constantly augmented by the higher Northern birthrate. Of course, Catholics could be persuaded to vote outside confessional lines, but until they did, either straying to support the fascists or the socialists, their party was in permanent ascendency. The Catholic Party itself adroitly accomplished the transition from arch-reactionary spokesmen of the needs of doctrine and the interests of a narrow upper stratum, to broadly-based middle-class party with cross-class support. Fundamentally the Flemish ascendency continued until the early nineteen-sixties, when the economic decline of Wallonia precipitated the sudden rise of trade union supported Walloon nationalism, which profoundly affected the political life of the nation.

In this context grew the socialist trade unions. The Belgian Labour Party was formed in 1885, and advocated a socialist programme from the beginning. A federation of trade union, co-operative and political bodies, it gave great stimulus to the formation of new co-operative and mutual aid societies, and as it grew, so did union membership. Trade unionism was radicalised by the extreme reluctance of the Belgian ruling class to yield political rights to the working people: in addition to the General Strike of 1893, the Party called similar strikes in 1902 and 1912 for the democratisation of the suffrage. It was during this period that Rosa Luxemburg said that European workers should 'learn to speak Belgian'. She was demanding the supple combination of direct action and parliamentary politics which evolved during the battle for an equal franchise. Once the male suffrage had been conceded on a basis of equality, in 1919, the socialists increased their parliamentary representation from 34 to 70, receiving more than 36% of the votes cast. This victory cost the still predominantly reactionary Catholic Party the majority it had held since 1884. A Catholic Socialist coalition ensued, and this produced notable social legislation, including the eight-hour day and a law permitting peaceful picketing in strikes. This coalition broke up when the socialists opted for opposition, and with a brief exception, they remained in opposition until the middle-thirties. The received structure had clearly settled to produce a permanent division at something near to parity, and it was only when the national movement in Flanders formally divided into socialist and fascist wings that the balance was disturbed to the point that Labour could win the largest number of Parliamentary seats. During this time Henri De Man developed his particular politics of 'revisionism' aimed at the conquest of middle-class support, while a powerful left-wing socialist current, headed by Paul-Henri Spaak, developed to the point at which its leader could enter the Cabinet and change his opinions. The political impasse continued with socialists in office, since no fundamental structural change was possible within the rules of the elaborate parliamentary game which had evolved. Socialist ministers reigned and equivocated while strikes on popular front scale spread out from France and erupted through the country, and the inevitable disillusionment which followed cost them their temporary political lead, before the Nazi invasion.

The invasion drove some socialist leaders into exile, while De Man remained behind and advocated the dissolution of the Labour Party, whose members, he advocated, should 'enter the cadres of national resurrection'.[5] Other more numerous activists chose the alternative course of resistance and sabotage, and this experience produced a radicalisation of the union militants, and a split in the Socialist federation, the then CGT. At the end of the Second World War, the

International Federation of Trade Unions sent a delegation to Brussels, Ghent, Liège and Antwerp and convened a representative conference in Brussels. They found four separate fractions among the unions: the old CGT leaders, the left-wing socialist breakaway CGT, the Communists and the Catholics. The IFTU spokesmen pushed for unification, and although they failed to bring the Catholics into a common federation, in 1945 the two wings of the socialist movement reunited. By September that year the new FGTB had won half a million members.[6] The FGTB gained its unity at the price of its integral membership of the socialist party, and from then on normally occupied a place to the left of the party in the political spectrum, whereas, before the war, the union had traditionally been largely to the right of the party. As Mandel has reported:

> 'The left wing was moulded by the strong personality of André Renard. This dynamic leader of the metalworkers of Liège had retained from his youth strong anarcho-syndicalist sympathies, and had little confidence in classic reformist policies, whether in Parliament or in wage negotiations with employers...he was able to forge the Liège unions into an extremely powerful weapon. On four separate occasions, in 1946, in 1948, in 1950 and in 1957, the strikes which he led at Liège wrested important concessions from employers and from succeeding governments, including governments with socialist participation'.[7]

Renard was the pioneer of the policy of 'Structural Reforms', which figured in the programme he presented in 1954 and again in 1956 at the FGTB Congresses.

'Structural Reform' is a slogan which has been interpreted in contradictory ways. In the hands of the Italian Communist Party it has meant little more than a policy of nationalisation and reforming legislation, with few significant differences from the sense of, say, the reform programme of the 1945 Labour Government in Britain. But in the strategy of the FGTB, 'structural reform' is at once a policy of mobilisation for change at the grass roots, and a series of coherent and specific demands on the legislature. It is therefore a realistic and genuinely radical programme since it is able, at the same time, to arouse the necessary social movement for socialist change and to pose the practical tests which any such radical movement must be able to apply to any body of its representatives. In this way, the Belgian trade unions had moved beyond the constricting formula of 'a minimum programme' of immediate reforms (higher pensions, more public housing, even some nationalsation) all bearing the scantest imaginable relationship to the ultimate goal of the socialist movement, which involves the libertarian transformation of all social relationships. The FGTB had reached a programmatic solution to an age-old problem for socialists everywhere, to wit, how to link their immediate demands with their dreams of the new society. The proposals contained a transitional element capable of arousing appetites and widening aspirations for change to the most audacious degree, yet always practical and down-to-earth. It was thus possible to envisage the overcoming of the inherent problem of socialists: that in the capitalist countries, socialists are divided into practical men who aim to change nothing substantial in society, and idealistic dreamers, who possess the *will* for change but wield none of the effective power to bring it about.

At the time that the FGTB embraced the cause of structural reform, the Socialist Party was engaged in an alliance with the Liberals, aimed at eroding Catholic influence by eating away public subsidies to Catholic schools.[8] The price of coalition with the Liberals was a freeze on all kinds of even mildly reforming actions, and had the FGTB accepted the strategy, they would have been outflanked on their left by the Catholic unions which in the circumstances could afford quite militant policies. The strategy was bound to be self-defeating on the electoral plane since it could only promote Catholic solidarity. But the fact that the FGTB rallied around an alternative programme produced a struggle within the Socialist Party in which the union-led caucus won a formal victory in 1958. At this point, the ambiguity in the structural reform programme became clear: after a verbal surrender, the socialist leaders evolved their own kind of 'structural' change involving no more than the kind of industrial rationalisation and indicative planning that became familiar, later, in Mr. Wilson's Britain. The Belgians were beguiled with all the rhetoric of incomes policy, and suffered many of the onslaughts of 'redeployment' before these wolves in sheeps' clothing were set loose in the British Labour Movement. In 1960 a great strike broke out over the introduction, by the Catholic Eyskens government, of a *loi unique* aimed at restoring an ailing economy at the expense of the working population. This general strike brought about the defeat of the Eyskens Administration, and the General Election which followed produced, yet again, another coalition. But in spite of the rhetoric of the socialist political leaders, no anti-capitalist structural reforms were forthcoming from this Government, no actions were taken against the holding companies in favour of extending trade union rights, and in the crisis of morale which afflicted the socialist ranks as a result the renewed upsurge of Walloon nationalism produced sharp conflicts and splits.[9]

All of this could only reinforce the lesson that the anti-capitalist content of structural reforms must be made abundantly plain, and the emphasis on workers' control as a key element in socialist strategy must be completely clear, if sufficient forces are ever to be assembled to insist upon the beginning of the transition to socialism. And it is this lesson which served to revive and intensify the keen discussion on workers' control within the FGTB.

The resultant programme remains a reform programme, whilst continuing the spirit of contestation and struggle. In it, the unions pin-point the vital need to maintain their autonomy of action, their initiative and their right to oppose. To this extent, the FGTB advances a genuine workers' control strategy, and not a policy of subordinate 'participation'. Naturally, all who see the struggle for economic democracy as an unremitting process, based upon the developing understanding of wider and wider sections of the working populace, confront the same dilemmas which are faced by the Belgian unions.

As their programme says:

'For the FGTB, participation necessarily implies the maintenance of union autonomy. It is in this context that we can describe workers' control in the following manner:

1. *Who?*
The FGTB considers that workers' control cannot be effected except by the workers organised into unions. Solidarity and cohesion amongst the workers in their unions is the guarantee of the defence of their interests: isolated workers cannot enjoy such benefits.

2. *When?*
The essential conditions for workers' control are that they should be informed in time, that is, that they should be informed previous to any decisions being taken and never be faced with a *fait accompli*.

3. *Of What?*

Of all the factors in any given economic and social situation. Thus it is not a matter of information limited to a few texts or other items, but on the contrary, the sum of elements must be presented to allow a rounded judgement of the situation.

4. *Why?*

So that there is the possibility (not the obligation) of exercising the right of dispute, that is to say, of presenting, if need be, our own alternative proposals. It is important to insist on the word 'possibility'; this means that the union reserves for itself the right to choose the time, the conditions, the duration and the issues with regard to which it might decide, completely autonomously, to exercise its right of dispute.

5. *On what levels?*

Workers' control must be exercised at all levels (enterprise, groups of enterprises, region, industrial sector, nation...) in close association with all the workers concerned.

6. *How is union freedom to be safeguarded?*

The union must at the same time safeguard its entire freedom of industrial action, its entire autonomy. The right of dispute does not only consist in safeguarding union autonomy, but also in promoting settlements which render this freedom of union activity technically possible.

Workers' control consists of continual limitation of arbitrary action on the part of the employers, thanks to measures permitting the intervention of the workers in areas which, previously, escaped them – by progressive conquests within the framework of the unions which preserve the autonomy of their rights and powers, which are continuously being renewed, assuring for the workers progressive mastery over economic and social life at all levels.

In a certain number of cases, management decisions concerning investment, for example, risk limiting the real margins for workers' claims. It is therefore essential for the unions to be able to advocate a settlement which re-establishes this margin for social progress.'[10]

It is always possible for groups, even large organisations, of workpeople to bargain for greater powers and then discover themselves wielding responsibilities which are larger than those powers warrant. 'Incorporation' is a constant snare. Yet advance cannot be made without running risks, and these risks can only be minimised if the unions remain open to correction by their members and sensitive to the complex problems involved in retaining the capacity for autonomous action. In a word, workers must control their unions before they can wrest even minimal advances in control over their work. But more: as the Belgian strategy makes plain, the unions need to operate on the level of the economy as well as that of the factory, and therefore require an effective political arm. So workers must control their parties before they can advance to control their economies. None of this is easy. And all the time, the employers and their political spokesmen can maintain cohesive organisations which have great flexibility and manipulate opinion through most of the modern brain-washing media.

Yet there is no alternative to this struggle other than surrender of all hopes for equality, all dreams of freedom. If workers prove incapable of controlling their own organisations, they remain manifestly unable to reach further afield. To the extent that their appetite for freedom is awakened, they can see the need for effective organisation to reach it. Of course, there is no guarantee that authority will allow a peaceful revolution to consolidate itself peacefully: but equally, there is not the slightest chance that the people will awaken in a violent revolution unless they are thwarted in the attempt to make a non-violent one. So that whether modern socialists place themselves in the 'physical force' or the 'moral force' camps of the industrial Charter, they cannot afford to by-pass the questions posed to them by the Belgian Trade Unions. In fact, as always, the working-class movement will, in Mao Tse-Tung's words, need to 'walk on two legs'. It will need direct action, on an ascending scale. It will need 'constitutional' reform, parliamentary enactment, on an ascending scale. It will need, to secure this combination of measures, the vision to define its goals and its strategy with the utmost clarity, and the will to unite to pursue them. In short, to re-echo Rosa Luxemburg, it will need to 'learn to speak Belgian' yet again, if socialism is ever to become a viable option in late-capitalist Europe.

First published in 1971

Footnotes
1. For a discussion of this process, see *European Political Parties:* P.E.P. Allen & Unwin, 1969, p.76 et seq.
2. Cf. Stephen Holt: *Six European States.* Hamish Hamilton, 1970, p.290.
3. Cf. Walter Kendall: Trade Unions in Belgium and Luxemburg, *European Community* 8-9, 1970, p.21 et seq.
4. Ernest Mandel: The Dialectic of Class and Region in Belgium, *New Left Review.* 20, p.6.
5. H. W. Laidler: *History of Socialism.* Routledge & Kegan Paul, 1968, p.494 et seq.
6. *Forty-Five Years – IFTU,* by Walter Schevenels. IFTU 1956.
7. Op. cit., p.21.
8. Op. cit.
9. Cf. Marcel Deneckere: How Can the Left Come to Power in Belgium? *International Socialist Journal,* no. *5-6, p.586* et seq.
10. Cf. *A Trade Union Strategy in the Common Market.* Spokesman Books, 1971.

9

Needs

An important part of the message of industrial democrats does, of course, turn on the need for representative forms of government. But an equally central strategy for democratic advance involves the establishment of an appropriate separation of powers, and information flows.

This essay was first published in The Spokesman *in 1976.*

The two related crises which have received a great deal of attention in the ecological debate raise the whole problem of popular participation in social planning to a new level of urgency. Both the acute depletion of certain non-renewable resources, and the aggravated difficulties of pollution and waste, have combined to cause men to question, ever more insistently, two things: the wisdom of allowing market forces to determine, unfettered, the rate of use of a scarce natural patrimony; and the implications of permitting entrepreneurs to cite the market as their alibi in order to avoid accusations of the systematic misapplication of materials, to say nothing of people. However, even before the recent growth of concern about the human environment, the demand for large extensions of democratic power was already becoming urgent.

During the postwar years, the growth of state intervention in the administration of privately controlled economies, with the concomitant increase in both publicly controlled enterprise and welfare provision of public services, has created large sectors of the advanced economies which are not necessarily crudely subordinate to market pressures, and which can, indeed, exert certain modest counter-influences within society, from time to time adversely affecting the free operation of the market. The result of this encroachment, however tentative and hesitant it may have been, has been a notable revival of concern with the concept of need, as distinct from the conventional economic notion of demand, which had dominated social thinking while the rationality of the market remained virtually unchallenged.[1]

The imagined sovereignty of 'demand' is obviously linked with the hegemony, or desired hegemony, of the market over all socio-economic decisions. The conventional distinction between 'effective' demand and its implied ghost, 'non-effective' demand, would be sheer nonsense within any strict interpretation of market-based economies, since the market must necessarily produce recognition of the human or social inadequacy of such models[2]. It has long been generally recognised, for instance, that market forces alone will never meet the housing needs, or the health needs, of large sectors of the populations working in even the most successful market economies. Since the market must necessarily produce an unequal distribution of income and wealth, there are always within its sway larger or lesser groups of people who lack the resources to translate some of their basic needs in these and other fields into 'effective demand'. Hence the growth of public provision, and of watchful underdog pressure groups in all the major economies. Orthodox economists were not always blind to these difficulties, and Marshall, for instance, troubled himself with the distinction not only between 'necessities' and other commodities, but also between the 'necessities of efficiency' and the necessities of existence.[3] But whilst all necessities were either provided in the marketplace or not at all, this remained an abstract preoccupation, and 'need' was condemned to seem a phantom idea outside the writings of utopians and socialists.

Today, in the self-styled Welfare States, the existence of a large infrastructure of local authority housing at more or less subsidised rents, of a free or poll-tax contributory health service, of extended facilities for public education, has revitalised the awareness of 'need' in distinction from, and often as opposed to, 'demand'. The Seebohm Report in Britain, for instance, gave semi-official status to the idea that 'the personal social services are large-scale experiments in ways of helping those in need'.[4]

Yet what is need? In the arguments of the current poverty lobby, and above all of the writers associated with the Child Poverty Action Group, there has been a consistent tendency to stress the learned nature of individual needs, and to worry away not only at Marshall's distinction between necessities of different kinds, but also at that between necessities and what other conventional economists call 'comforts' or even 'luxuries'. Undoubtedly the material basis for such a sustained intellectual offensive has been the non-market area of publicly provided social security.

A French study has made an effort to quantify the growth of this public sector of need-provision. CREDOC, the Centre for Research and Documentation of Consumer Affairs, identified three kinds of need: elementary needs, such as food, clothing, toiletries, etc; environmental needs, such as housing, leisure, transport; and 'needs related to the person', such as education, sports, health, cultural provision. They then attempted to aggregate the expenditures in each category which were made in the open market, the costs of freely provided public services, and those other costs which were refunded by social security services.[5] Their findings offer an interesting perspective on the subject:

	1959		1970	
	Collective Share %	Private Share %	C/S %	P/S %
Elementary	00	100	00	100
Environmental	10	90	12.5	87.5
Person	54	46	68	32
All Services	12	88	19	81

Of course, many questions remain to be asked within this framework. We cannot assume that these expenditures are uniform for all social groups, and the variations between one group and another can tell us extremely significant things about the social structure concerned.

What remains very plain is that public provision, taken at its own valuation, has different motors from market-oriented production. Commonly the social services 'create' or 'discover' needs which hitherto had never been imagined by the governors of society, and possibly not even by some of the beneficiaries of the process. In the field of adult education, poor as it is in endowments, this is a truism. But it can also be held relevant in many other areas. In the newly formed British National Health Service, the original heavy demands for false teeth and spectacles triggered off a celebrated public controversy, once these items became freely available. It was argued at the time that this rush for aid reflected the privation previously imposed by the system of market provision on those too poor (or too mean) to exercise 'effective demand'. But in a similar way, the elaboration of medical technology constantly creates new and newer needs, some of them involving far more investment than teeth and glasses. No one could 'need' a kidney machine until there was one.

An interesting example of this process is to be found in the case of speech therapy. Roughly half a million people in Britain stammer (0.8% of the population). It has been calculated that perhaps 400,000 of these people are seriously afflicted. There are 900 full-time and 500 part-time speech therapists. A recent enquiry, published in the *The Guardian*, asked 30 Local Education Authorities how many adult classes they held for adult stammerers. There were three adult evening classes, two in Lancashire and one in the South of England. As Mr. Muirden, the author of this study, points out:

'This educational development is, therefore, in the hands of local stammerers and potential tutors, who must come out of their individual nonentity and organise themselves into a recognisable body.'[6]

'Need' that is to say, is not merely learned by imitation and diffused by social osmosis: awareness of it can be consciously communicated, the more so when remedies are on hand, but also to some extent when they are technically possible even if not actually available.

Yet this raises vast problems about the allocation of scarce resources. Nottinghamshire County Council recently attracted serious adverse criticism when they appointed a teacher who was subsequently denigrated as a 'Pocket-money Advisor' to organise consumer advice for children in schools. The appointment was, of course, open to debate: although some at least of the consumer groups would have welcomed it. The question is, by what criteria should such decisions be made? How does one hitherto unrecognised 'need' secure priority over another? Who decides, subject to what community controls?

Gunnar Myrdal, in his interesting study *Beyond the Welfare State*,[7] points out that the institutions of welfare in the West have grown up in a democratic environment in distinction from the mechanisms of planning in the USSR and other communist governed countries, which came into existence in the context of an authoritarian political framework. Unfortunately, the soil in which welfare has grown does not mean that it necessarily retains democratic properties itself. We have hardly succeeded in rendering the public social services democratic in themselves, either in the sense of asserting direct popular participation in, and control of them; or in the more fundamental and indispensable sense of subjecting them to effective and satisfying detailed public accountability.

Part of the problem can be seen in one of the most interesting studies of the taxonomy of need, published in *New Society* by Jonathan Bradshaw.[8] Bradshaw is rightly concerned about the amorphousness of the concepts of need, and in an effort towards clarity separates four distinct definitions.

First, he identifies the idea of normative need, which may be summarised as the bureaucratic determination, by an administration of social scientists, of minimum levels of adequacy. These norms may be matched by remedial provision, or they may not. Examples he offers include the British Medical Association's nutritional standard, or Peter Townsend's 'incapacity scale'. Much progress has been made in defining such norms in the fields of housing and education during recent years.

Secondly, he recognises felt need, as the stated wants of those for whom services are offered.

Thirdly, he lists expressed need, or demand (not in the economic sense) in which lacks will provoke actions, demanding a service. Examples he offers include hospital waiting lists, or possibly, housing waiting lists.

Finally, he accepts the idea of comparative need, in which either persons or areas are compared with others, and found to lack amenities which are generally accepted as necessary elsewhere.

Bradshaw then goes on to offer a model connecting these different concepts which can interrelate those more or less precise measures of need which may be elaborated on the basis of each taken individually. The important thing about this whole valuable exercise is that it is oriented at planners and policy-makers exclusively, to enable them to refine and evaluate their judgements. And it is exactly this 'need' of the planners which demonstrates how far our services are from being able to live up to Gunnar Myrdal's expectations about their 'democratic' content, since effective participation and consultation would by themselves produce notable refinements in most public plans, as well as allowing planners to educate themselves in the process.

The relevance of this problem to the wider ecological issues, demanding as they do significant extensions of planning, both in order to eke out scarce materials, to research and develop substitutes, and to clear up and prevent mess, should be evident. Democratic forms of society will be increasingly difficult to maintain unless we can effectively extend the principles of social accountability and direct popular participation in decision-taking into what are, at present, either authoritarian or technocratic preserves. Naturally, this is not to argue against the development of technique, now more urgent than ever, but to argue for its application under genuinely democratic controls, in response to democratic initiatives.

At this point, one must obviously consider the tools which are available for such controls. The growth of governmental and local administrative organs, voluntary organisations, trade unions, and pressure groups certainly provides us with a confusion of institutions. What is required is not simply a refinement of organisational forms, still less a proliferation of offices, but an enrichment of the simple traditional constitutional doctrine of separation of powers, such as might prove possible once we began to take the notion of accountability seriously. Any genuine separation of powers exists to prevent the concentration of authority in a manner harmful to civil liberties. Bitter experience, in a succession of countries, reveals the peril of minimising the importance of the continuous extension of such checks and controls, to render them relevant and effective to cope with the enormous (and up to now, largely necessary) growth of bureaucratic administrative forms.

In its pure form, this problem poses itself most clearly in the 'socialist' societies, in which planning is unimpeded by the institutions of private property, yet in which democratic initiatives are as yet markedly limited and, indeed, restricted. This has been perceptively understood by Mihailo Markovic (the Yugoslav scholar who was dismissed, with his colleagues in the Belgrade School of Philosophy, after an unprecedented governmental campaign which culminated in an arbitrary decision by the state authorities of Serbia to overrule the University's statutes. At the beginning of 1975, against the will of their colleagues, the Belgrade philosophers were suspended from teaching duties).

Markovic argues[9] that the doctrine of separation of powers needs now to be consciously applied to information and communication services, so that not only raw data, but also access to competent, and if necessary, adversary, technical advice, should become available to groups of citizens as of right, for whatever social purposes might seem relevant to them.

In capitalist economies, the resistance to such doctrines has a dual root, in contrast to the single, bureaucratic-political source of limitations on information flows which control the communist states. Capitalist societies encourage a certain dissociated pluralism in the communications media, and in the fields of intellectual organisation: although they have given rise to a modified bureaucracy in both local and national government and their out-stations, which is not without its East European parallel. But the major obstacle to freedom of information is still, in such societies, undoubtedly located in the institutions of private property, which require that not only material producer goods, but certain kinds of knowledge, be restricted to more or less exclusive proprietorship. To establish truly universal access to knowledge would be to negate the domination of resources by particular interests: and it is this salient fact which has encouraged the industrial demand for accountability, commonly pursued under the slogan 'open the books'.[10]

Needless to say, this is not to argue that universal access to knowledge can be achieved without other prior material changes. George Orwell pin-pointed this question with characteristic clarity when he wrote that: 'Until they become conscious they will never rebel, and until after they have rebelled they cannot become conscious.'[11] While the problem is confined solely to human consciousness, it is insoluble.

In industry, the grassroots urge for access to information has been reflected in official programmes adopted by both the British Labour Party[12] and the Trades Union Congress.[13] The whole strategy of 'planning agreements', as devised in the Party's industrial policy statements, was originally conceived as a two-way squeeze on private monopolies of information, from trade union and governmental sides respectively.[14] Companies would be compelled to disclose certain whole categories of information, both to the state and their own employees (through the unions), thus facilitating both collective bargaining and tripartite planning decisions. In the event, the Wilson administration discreetly withdrew from the honouring of this commitment, but, instead, adopted parts of the institutional framework which had been proposed by the Labour Party in opposition, carefully filleting this of the real powers which had been intended for it.

But whilst the Government has chosen caution, the grassroots organisations of the trade unions have shown increasing belligerence on this question. One of the main by-products of the movement of factory occupations, which began at Upper Clyde Shipbuilders, was the development of the notion of the 'social audit'.[15] Originally canvassed as a response to pit closures during the 1960s, this idea came to life in a most spectacular way, when the Scottish TUC convened an extended public enquiry into the overall socio-economic effects of the proposed closure of the shipyards. Naturally, the balance sheets of UCS provided many arguments for closure. But, taken in conjunction with the social costs of unemployment, re-housing and renovation of industrial potential, these arguments became much less convincing. A wider accounting framework posed questions which could never even be asked within a straightforward calculation of profit and loss within the shipbuilding industry itself. Even excluding the moral costs of closure, which is itself a moral choice which may or may not be justified, the simple cash costs of social security benefits and redevelopment could, when carefully computed, provide powerful evidence for maintaining an otherwise 'unprofitable' concern in being. The example of the Scottish TUC was subsequently emulated in a number of other threatened enterprises. At the River Don Steelworks in Sheffield, white-collar and production workers combined to produce a blueprint of the effects of closure proposals which aroused widespread concern amongst industrialists who were British Steel Corporation customers, and resulted in effective pressure for a stay of execution. By the time that the 1974 Wilson administration took office, this kind of reasoning had taken root very widely, and the new industry minister, Mr. Tony Benn, found it perfectly possible to encourage its more general application.

Confronted by a widespread liquidity crisis, British industry was facing a particularly difficult time. Not only were there bankruptcies and closures of plants on a wide scale, but a number of transnational companies were brought to the point at which they decided to close all or part of their British production potential, and to opt for attempts to hold their previous market shares by importing products from their overseas plants. Tony Benn greeted the workers' representatives who besieged him for governmental help in these situations with a novel proposal: he commissioned independent consultants to prepare feasibility studies under the control and guidance of the relevant trade union bodies. This innovation was applied in cases such as the closure of Imperial Typewriters' factories in Leicester and Hull:[16] it stimulated the unions into complex efforts at alternative planning. Not only did they have to argue with qualified professionals about the possibilities of continued or modified production in the plants concerned: they were also powerfully motivated to examine the overall performance of their former employers, to document the investment and marketing programmes which had produced their present adversity, and to seek to arouse public discussion on the social priorities involved.

The demotion of Mr. Benn after the result of the EEC referendum was not sufficient to prevent the continuance of this type of approach. When Chrysler Motors announced their closure plans towards the end of 1975,[17] the instant response of the shop stewards was to replicate this example, in a most careful and imaginative way. Perhaps the most dramatic example of the social audit at work is to be found in the extraordinary initiative of Lucas Aerospace workers[18] who, encouraged by Mr. Benn, prepared a detailed blueprint for the transfer of their industry to 'socially useful and necessary projects'.

Naturally, the social audit has, until now, remained mainly a labour of self-education and, in a sense, propaganda. But it is not difficult to see the potential which it contains as an instrument for democratic planning. By putting experts to work for oppositional groups, it calls in question the prerogatives of managers and professional planners, and ends the monopoly of initiative.

If the welfare sectors of our economy were to learn from these experiments, they could rapidly extend their innovative capacity in a very real way. If the social audit is relevant to productive effort, then its correlative in the field of social consumption would be the 'needs budget' or inventory of social demands.[19] There is nothing to stop local authorities, or welfare agencies, from initiating an open and continuous discussion upon the question of which needs should have priority, and how scales of priority would be determined. This could enfranchise all the welfare pressure groups, and bring them into an organised effort to evaluate the relative importance of their own particular claims on public resources. As things are, most bureaucracies calculate their future development in terms of x per cent expansion across the board in favourable times, and y per cent cuts during the lean years. A rudimentary jockeying can take place between departments, but it is no secret that the outcome of this is frequently determined as much by the personal capacities of the jockeys as by the comparative urgency of the needs upon which they ride. If needs budgets became as general a feature of the work of such agencies as their normal revenue and expenditure accounts, then the process of popular consultation and discussion which would be involved would itself constitute a real resource, which could itself help to expand the material means which were available to solve specific problems.

In the middle run, such democratic advances as the social audit and the needs budget will prove themselves necessary if there is to be any future for democratic political forms in general. The capitalist industrial powers have advanced half-way to democracy, but if there is not a continued forward movement there will be a retreat. Half-and-half autocracy and self-government is no permanent mixture: it is, in our situation, an impasse, in which government of any kind, leave alone self-government, becomes increasingly impossible.

If we are to consider that the debate on the environment has warned us of real hazards, we must anticipate attempts to discover authoritarian solutions for them. The alternative, which perhaps begins with the kind of tentative reforms outlined here, will see needs as growing in an increasingly self-aware social process, and will seek to meet them by recognising their combined personal and social identity. This task could never be begun outside an ever-expanding democracy.

First published in 1976

Footnotes

1. Cf. notably Peter Townsend: The Meaning of Poverty, reprinted in his collection *The Social Minority* (p.35 et seq.), Allen Lane, 1973. Also two essays by the same author in *The Concept of Poverty*, Heinemann, 1970.

2. Recently this recognition has been extended, as city governments themselves have met mounting financial pressures. Cf. Theodore W. Kheel: The Quality of Regional Development – The Case of New York, in *Qualitat des Lebens*, 6: Europaische Verlagsanstalt, Frankfurt 1972.

3. Alfred Marshall: *Principles of Economics, Vol I*, p.122. See also Charles S. Wyand: *The Economics of Consumption*, Macmillan N.Y., 1937, Chapter 5.

4. Even so, the Seebohm Report provided no satisfactory definition of 'need'.

5. Bernard Cazes: Planning for the Quality of Life in Mixed Economies, in *Qualitat des Lebens*, 7: Europaische Verlagsanstalt, Frankfurt 1972.

6. Ronald Muirden is Tutor in Stammering Correction at the Addison and Central London Institutes, and author of *Stammering Correction Simplified*, (I. Garnett Miller Limited, London).

7. Duckworth, 1960. Cf. Chapters 7 and 8 especially.

8. 30th March, 1972. No. 496, pp.640-3.

9. In an as yet unpublished paper to the American Philosophical Society, 1975 Convention.

10. Cf. Michael Barratt Brown: *Opening the Books*. IWC Pamphlet No. 4, 1968.

11. *1984*, Penguin Edition, p.60.

12. The Labour Party: *Report on Industrial Democracy*, June 1967 and *Labour's Programme, 1973*.

13. TUC: *Interim Report on Industrial Democracy*, 1975: and *Report on Industrial Democracy*, 1974.

14. See Stuart Holland: *Strategy for Socialism*, Spokesman Books 1975, pp.62-76, and the same author's *The Socialist Challenge*, Quartet books 1975, chapters 7,8, 10 and 11.

15. Michael Barratt Brown: *UCS: The Social Audit*, IWC Pamphlet No. 26, 1971.

16. *Why Imperial Typewriters Must Not Close*: IWC Pamphlet No. 46, 1975.

17. Joint Union Declaration of Chrysler Shop Stewards and Staff Representatives: *Chrysler's Crisis: The Workers' Answer*, December 8th 1975.

18. Lucas Aerospace Combine Shop Steward Committee: *Corporate Plan*, 1976, published by E. F. Scarbrow, Hayes, Middlesex.

19. Cf. my paper *The Social Audit* and the Inventory of Social Needs, in *Community Development Journal*, OUP, Volume 8, No. 3, October 1973.

10
Wilson Sets Up a Commission

In accordance with various election pledges the Wilson Government established a Committee of Enquiry under the chairmanship of Lord Bullock. Its terms of reference were as follows: 'Accepting the need for a radical extension of industrial democracy in the control of companies by means of representation on boards of directors, and accepting the essential role of trade union organisations in this process to consider how such an extension can best be achieved, taking into account in particular the proposals of the Trades Union Congress report on industrial democracy as well as experience in Britain, the EEC and other countries. Having regard to the interest of the national economy, employees, investors and consumers, to analyse the implications of such representation for the efficient management of companies and for company law.'

Bullock's overall agenda helped to colour his report, which recommended the establishment of company boards composed of equal numbers of worker directors and shareholder representatives, mediated by a third group of mutually agreeable technical appointments. This was the famous '2x + y' formula, which turned on the feasibility of reaching agreement between the two contending blocks of worker and shareholder representatives as to who might make up the intermediary 'y' group.

Tony Topham and I published a detailed analysis of the Bullock Report as a Shop Stewards' Guide. *This appeared later in 1977, and was published by Spokesman Books. This article appeared in the* Bulletin *of the IWC, February/March 1976.*

The October 1974 Election Manifesto, upon which the present Government returned to office, contained an explicit pledge to honour the decisions previously reached in a series of Labour Party Conferences.

> "We will" it said, "introduce new legislation to help forward our plans for a radical extension of industrial democracy in both the private and public sectors. This will involve major changes in company law and in the statutes which govern the nationalised industries and the public services."

Already in February 1974, the previous Manifesto had pledged:

"We intend to socialise the nationalised industries. In consultation with the unions, we shall take steps to make the management of existing nationalised industries more responsible to the workers in the industry and more responsive to their consumers' needs."

This is the context in which the newly appointed Commission on Industrial Democracy has begun to work. Charged to report within a year, and seeking written evidence before March, it *seems* to be in a hurry, and this could be taken as an earnest that legislation is intended during the current Parliament. No doubt that impression was intended: but it would be naïve to accept that it accords with the likely future.

Commissions of Enquiry, in the given political system, can be set up wherever there are technical complexities requiring legislative treatment, or, alternatively, where contentious issues need resolution. In this second case, the function of a Commission may be to resolve antagonistic interests, or to simply provide an excuse for delay...

First published in 1976

11

The Case for Consumer Democracy

With the establishment of the Bullock Committee, and its enquiry into Industrial Democracy, the debate began to extend itself into the established news media. For a long time, our conversations about democratic reform had taken place, as it were, on the margins of official society in workshops and meetings of a few hundred more or less like-minded individuals. But now, all the great organs of official opinion were commissioning their commentaries.

Often these were not well-versed in the ideas of industrial democracy, which were commonly deemed to be simplistic, and therefore suitable for the unsophisticated. In fact, all the complexities of democratic thought were, if anything, further complicated by efforts to make it relevant to industrial life.

These afforded an opportunity for me to enter the discussion in The Times. *The Case for Consumer Democracy first appeared in 1976.*

In their evidence to the Bullock Committee, which is examining the TUC's proposals for the reform of company structure, the National Consumer Council suggests that, if unions are to be represented on company boards, then consumers must be represented as well. The council echoes Sidney and Beatrice Webb in suggesting a tripartite system of government for nationalised industries, involving 'consumers, employees and management': and they suggest that if Lord Bullock recommends in favour of union representatives on the supervisory boards of ordinary companies, then they will need to campaign for similar facilities for consumers. This view seems to have influenced Ronald Butt, in his discussion of workers' control *(The Times,* April 29, 1976).

Advocates of industrial democracy will tend to agree that any balanced reform of the industrial power structure must augment the effective powers of consumers: although few would now defend the proposals of the Webbs as offering any practical advantage either to individual consumers or to effective management. Yet undoubtedly, those of us who wish to see an extension of workers' control have a responsibility to think through the problem of the defence of consumer interests.

In order to do this, it is necessary to question the assumption, shared by Mr. Butt and the National Consumer Council, that industrial democracy necessarily amounts either to 'syndicalism' or neo-syndicalism. The weakness of anarcho-syndicalism as a model for social organisation was that it sought to enfranchise labour by giving over the government of industry and society to industrially organised unions, which, it proposed, would administer industry within a market framework. It was difficult to see how this arrangement could facilitate either social planning, or the development of social forms of consumption.

The current rediscovery of the ideals of self-management and workers' control takes place in a context in which the negative lessons of omnipotent state bureaucracy are completely plain to read, while the western capitalist economies have evolved very large welfare sectors practising highly social forms of distribution (as in the health and education services, where there already exists in several countries something close to distribution according to need); and a variety of experiments in indicative planning, some of which, with the aid of devices such as planning agreements, could actually be transformed into effective prescriptive planning mechanisms, subject to a high degree of democratic accountability. In this situation, the key weaknesses of syndicalism are considerably limited, if not entirely overcome. In great measure, we have in planning structures the solution to the problem of representing firms in their capacities as consumers.

If consumer democracy is to become real, in the form of personal powers as well as collective ones, it seems urgent to look at a wider range of democratic approaches than are involved in simple representation. Direct representation is possible wherever there are constituencies close-knit enough both to constitute an electorate and provide an active and continuing public opinion capable of influencing, and holding accountable, such representatives as are chosen. A coal mine, for instance, is exactly comparable with the units which seemed logical to the Greeks for the practice of democracy. But coal consumers fall into two categories: on one side, the large customers, pre-eminently power stations, and, on the other, a dwindling band of personal users of solid fuel. The first category of consumers are certainly compact enough to be involved in the National Coal Board, although they are likely to find their interests better served if adequate inter-industrial planning machinery can be evolved. The individual coal burner, however, is a constituent of a territory so amorphous that it is impossible to see how he could be democratically represented. How could he vote, and how would his delegate discover his views? Does this mean, therefore, that he may have no democratic rights or influence? Not at all.

The device which he needs to develop will be an extension of the old constitutional doctrine of the separation of powers. He needs access to objective information, and the means to contribute his own information, including, of course, complaints, to the stock of such knowledge. The dissemination and collection of such information needs to be organised, and kept as rigorously separate from executive authority as the judiciary, and yet it needs to have inviolable rights of access to the facts which are relevant to it. Free public opinion will sooner or later do the rest. If *Which?* reports that a given car is twice as costly and half as efficient as its competitors, then its manufacturers, whether they are organised in autocratic or democratic units, will have to pay attention. If the consumer defenders report that a given toy is dangerous to children, then the lobby can even, if necessary, seek legislative action to prevent its distribution. The principle can be extended to the point at which consumers feel that they are satisfied: and today 'consumers' may include numbers of socially conscious and quarrelsome defenders of the environment

Direct representation would, of course, be eminently feasible in the area of social, as opposed to individual, consumption. Already we have lay governors of schools, and public nominees serve in the controlling bodies of a variety of welfare agencies. Yet, even in this sector, perhaps the doctrine of separation of powers has greater relevance than the mechanism of representation. If our major public services were compelled to operate a public, open, and active needs budget, involving an ongoing institutionalised discussion between all the relevant pressure groups, then not only could priorities be rationally tabled and independently assessed, but quite possibly considerable scope could be given to stimulating voluntary efforts within the public sector. Were an advisory needs budget part of the local government mechanism, such problems would be ventilated, and the process of accountability would be markedly improved.

In short, if we want to apply democratic norms to economic institutions, we have far more scope than might be thought by those who confine themselves to the narrow agenda suggested by the issue of representation. Workgroups can and should be served by representative forms of government: but that government need be no less constrained by overall democratic pressures than any other. An industrial democracy will need to carry the doctrine of separation of powers to hitherto undreamt of limits.

First published in 1976

12

Workers' Producer Co-operatives

Following the Upper Clyde Shipbuilders' work-in, a large number of experiments took place with the establishment of co-operative producers' associations. Many of these were subsequently described in a book called The New Worker Co-operatives, *published in 1976 by Spokesman. Some of the new producer co-ops were fostered by Tony Benn, until he was removed from the position of Secretary of State for Industry. His successor, Eric Varley, showed no enthusiasm for such experiments, although the Institute for Workers' Control continued to offer help and advice to groups of workers who sought it. This was an introductory chapter to* The New Worker Co-operatives.

Although the creation of workers' producer co-operatives was a relatively late development in the upsurge of factory occupations in Britain which took place after the 1971 work-in at Upper Clyde Shipbuilders, arguments about whether co-operative production might be possible broke out in many of the earlier sit-ins, and were mainly discouraged by the political groupings who flocked around to offer advice and support. It often seems a 'natural' response to an active trade unionist, once he has begun to doubt the permanence of the relationship of employer-employee itself, rather than raising the simpler problem of shifting given terms of employment in his favour, to begin to consider some form of localised or co-operative self-management. Factory occupations encouraged precisely such questioning. As they became more and more common, the questions they posed to their participants became more insistent. Between July 1971 and March 1974 one researcher was able to count 102 distinct occupations, a large proportion of which were initiated in defence of employment.[1]

The first such occupation to result in the formation of a co-operative producer's association was a special case. At Fakenham, in Norfolk, a small group of women leather workers, belonging to a very conservative trade union, the National Union of Footwear, Leather and Allied Trades, took over their little factory in order to resist its closure. After a 17-week long work-in, they were able to secure financial backing from the Scott Bader Commonwealth (a successful common ownership organisation operating a chemical factory at Wellingborough) and to establish their own self-managed company in new premises.[2] During the occupation the women manufactured suede dresses and hand-bags which they were able to sell through volunteers, many of whom came forward from the Women's Liberation Movement. In spite of strong hostility from the Executive Committee of their trade union, they received considerable support from their fellow-members, and were able to secure publicity on a national scale.

Operating as they did in a labour-intensive business, their capital requirements were quite modest and well within the means of an established organisation such as Scott Bader. The initial loan given to the women was £2,500. As the new co-operative extended itself, the workforce grew from 10 to 30 and Scott Bader successively provided further loans, totalling £10,000 over three years. After an initial experiment in diversification, the women took on a professional manager and agreed to concentrate on manufacturing uppers for shoes, and this degree of specialisation brought them into considerable difficulty when the shoe industry entered another recession in 1975. But the Fakenham experiment helped to draw attention to a time-honoured prescription for industrial democracy: and even in work-ins and sit-ins where the co-operative option was far more difficult to realise, there were voices raised in its favour. For instance, at the Briant Colour Printing work-in, which attracted widespread support for what became a very militant dispute, there were apparently insistent calls to explore the possibility of establishing a co-operative,[3] which were voted down on the recommendation of the work-in's leaders.

At Leadgate Engineering, at Durham in the North of England, another co-operative (known as Nightsbridge Ltd.) was established, with the help of the parent company which had been compelled to reconsider its original decision to close its Durham plant by the resultant six-month sit-in. This company, Stibbe & Co., was a hosiery firm based in Leicester, which controlled a number of subsidiary plants engaged in the manufacture of hosiery machinery. It had hoped to transfer the machinery from its Durham factory to another closer to HQ. When it agreed to recognise the rights of the labour force (which it had unsuccessfully declared redundant) to form a co-operative, it negotiated a contract under which it would agree to purchase the hosiery machinery manufactured by the new enterprise.[4] This situation raised one of the most common arguments about the difficulties of the co-operative strategy: it differed little from the old trade union device of the 'collective contract', which, for various reasons, aroused suspicion among some modern trade unionists.

The real breakthrough in co-operative forms of organisation, however, came with the election of the February 1974 Labour Government, which brought Mr. Anthony Wedgwood Benn back to the office of Secretary of State for Industry. Mr. Benn inherited a variety of problems of factory closure, in a general liquidity crisis which was rapidly inducing bankruptcies in numerous parts of British manufacturing industry. At the time he came to office, there was a major dispute running in the motor cycle industry, where the Norton Villiers Triumph factory at Meriden was under occupation by at least 250 of the original 1750 workers who had been declared redundant in a programme of reorganisation initiated by the owners of the plant, who were concentrating motor-cycle production in their Birmingham factory at Small Heath. Meriden was soon to be joined by other occupations.

In July of that year, 1200 workers at the former Fisher-Bendix factory at Merseyside, which had already been the scene of a prolonged sit-in in 1972, and which had resulted in a temporarily successful rescue operation, found their plant on the edge of disaster. They were informed that extensive lay-offs were necessary and that a maximum of 450 jobs could be rescued. Refusing to accept this kind of surgery, they once again occupied the factory and brought the question to the attention of Mr. Benn. Earlier, in March, the offices of the *Scottish Daily Express* in Glasgow had been closed by the proprietors, Beaverbrook Newspapers, in order to concentrate their efforts on extending the sales of the English editions. 1800 workers were made redundant, and a thousand of them voted to sit-in. Approaches to Mr. Peter Shore, the Secretary for Trade in their newly-elected government, did not succeed in saving the newspaper as it stood, but did elicit a promise that the government would look at proposals for a workers' co-operative, which might be able to produce a Scottish daily newspaper in the abandoned plant.

After what seem to have been extensive arguments within the government, Mr. Benn was able to persuade it to endorse plans to finance workers' co-operatives in each of these three enterprises. The government agreed to lend £3.9m to the former Fisher-Bendix (IPD) factory, which was to resume operations under the name of the Kirkby Manufacturing & Engineering Company. Of this sum, £1.8m was needed to pay off the Receiver in order to clear the liabilities of the old company. The government also agreed to put up almost £5m for the Meriden motor-cycle factory, and to offer £1.75m to the workers' co-operative at what was to become the *Scottish Daily News*, on condition that they raised the balance of the necessary capital. £250,000 had already been collected in personal contributions from the redundant workers, who contributed their severance pay. Half-a-million pounds had to be raised in unsecured loans, and £775,000 from secured loans.

After considerable difficulties each of these co-operatives was successful in establishing itself. None became registered under the legislation governing the formation of co-operative societies, for a variety of technical and legal reasons. All chose instead to register as companies under the Companies Act, having provided themselves with Statutes, Memoranda and Articles of Association which enjoined the strictest participating democracy.

*   *   *

The reaction of socialists to these developments was mixed. Whilst many trade unionists found the new developments to be exciting, the socialist groups tended to be highly sceptical. In July, 1974, the *Socialist Worker* launched an editorial broadside against the new co-operatives:

> 'What is the correct policy to fight closures? First, of course, a refusal to accept the management decision. Then the takeover of the plant to get the leverage to make the refusal matter. But what then?
> Two cases going on now are instructive. At the *Scottish Daily Express* in

Glasgow, the employer, Beaverbrook Newspapers, offered to sell the plant to the workers – more exactly to give them first refusal provided they raised enough money to meet the asking price.

The cash was to come from redundancy pay, government money, if possible and collections. The paper would then be relaunched under workers' management. It looks as though this scheme will fall through for lack of enough money. But suppose it had succeeded, would it have solved the problem?

The object is to save jobs. The running of a newspaper, or any other enterprise, along commercial lines requires that commercial considerations come first. Workers' management sounds attractive but that management would face the same problems as the Beaverbrook management.

It would have to try to solve them by trimming the workforce, by jacking up productivity, by pushing "flexibility" and generally undermining the conditions that union action has achieved in the industry. On top of all this, in the newspaper industry there is the conflict between the politics of a "workers' management" newspaper and the demands of the advertisers.

Of course it may be argued that the old management was incompetent, that the workers can do it better. Probably. But this does not alter anything fundamental.

You cannot build islands of socialism in a sea of capitalism. And workers' management of a commercial concern operating in that sea deprives the workers of the strength of union organisation directed against management. The National Union of Journalists has now recognised this and has adopted, in words at any rate, the correct demand: nationalise to save the jobs.'[5]

The initial response of the Communist Party's *Morning Star* to the Meriden workers' attempts to raise funding for a co-operative was also critical. Subsequently the Industrial Organiser of the Communist Party, Mr. Bert Ramelson, in a statement to the Executive Committee of the Party, during Spring 1975, revised this attitude, saying that co-operatives were a form of partial democracy.

A very plain and clear statement of the grounds for opposition to new co-operative experiments was made by Ernest Mandel, the Marxist economist who is one of the leaders of the Fourth International. Writing in the English journal *International*, he said:

'Not only is self-management limited to the level of the factory, workshop or assembly line, an illusion from an economic point of view, in that the workers cannot implement decisions taken at this level against the operations of market laws, but, worse still, the decisions taken by the workers become more and more exclusively restricted to decisions about profits, as can be clearly seen in Yugoslavia. The fundamental principle underlying self-management, which is the liberation of labour, whereby workers dominate the process of production, decide for themselves the speed of the assembly line and the organisation of work in the factory, and which is part and parcel of the sort of socialist society we are trying to build, is unrealisable in an economy which allows the survival of competition.

As the Yugoslav example shows only too clearly, the survival of competition imposes certain unavoidable imperatives on the units of production. They are faced with an unenviable decision. On the one hand, they can accept the logic of rationalisations: reduction of the labour force, speed-up, and so on. On the other, they can reject this logic, thus condemning certain units of production to operate at a loss and to pay wages far below average rates.

The only solution to all these questions is to regulate industry at a social level, thus allowing for an effectively planned economy consciously run by the working class as a whole, and for the process of deproletarianisation to advance.

The basis of the problem which I have attempted to elucidate is, thus, quite simple: for us, the notion of the class power of the proletariat exists in a very real sense precisely as class power and not the power of groups. To a large extent, these two conceptions are mutually exclusive. The more power is given to groups, the less is the power of the class as it is split into groups fighting amongst themselves.

So here we have another consequence of the reintroduction of competition on the road to socialism: given a market economy and autonomous decision making by productive units, there will be competition with groups of workers from different factories competing with each other, often very fiercely. From the outset factories do not have the same productivity so, if they compete with each other and each factory retains what it calls the "fruits of its labour", what it is in fact keeping is its revenue determined by its initial financial situation. Whether its initial endowment in terms of fixed capital, tools, machinery, equipment and even local situation was a matter of luck or of social factors, there is no possible justification for those who are fortunate enough to work in above average factories to employ an economic advantage over those who are employed in below average factories.

If the decision-making and advantages of each particular factory are left to the workers of that factory to deal with (even if, as in the case of Yugoslavia, a token "national solidarity tax" is levied), a situation of blatant inequality is created within the working-class, and when there exist blatant inequalities, it follows that the collective struggle of the working class as a whole for its common interests is broken down by the internecine struggles of different groups of workers.

It is, thus, to deceive the workers to lead them to believe that they can manage their affairs at the level of the factory. In the present economic system, a whole series of decisions are inevitably taken at higher levels than the factory, and if these decisions are not consciously made by the working class as a whole, then they will be made by other forces in society behind the workers' backs.'[6]

These criticisms are not groundless, and it is worth exploring them in some detail. To begin with, it is of course true that the market-mechanism must constantly be in tension with any elements of industrial democracy whatever. Over long periods of time the process of democratisation must be seen as a process of limitation, and ultimately of annulment, of blind market powers. We owe this insight to Karl Marx above all, and it remains sharply valid.

Yet it is interesting to contrast the nuanced and, in general, enthusiastic support which was offered by Marx to the co-operatives of his own day, with the dismissive attitude of his later followers to the new co-operative experiments of a vastly different time. In mid-1866 the Provisional General Council of the International Working Men's Association adopted as its own report to the Geneva Congress of the International this statement by Marx himself:

'It is the business of the International Working Men's Association to combine and generalise the spontaneous movements of the working classes, but not to dictate or impose any doctrinary system whatever. The Congress should, therefore, proclaim no special system of cooperation, but limit itself to the enunciation of a few general principles.

(a) We acknowledge the co-operative movement as one of the transforming forces of the present society based on class antagonism. Its great merit is to practically show that the present pauperizing and despotic system of the subordination of labour to capital can be superseded by the republican and beneficent system of the association of free and equal producers.

(b) Restricted, however, to the dwarfish forms into which individual wages-slaves can elaborate it by their private efforts, the co-operative system will never transform capitalistic society. To convert social production into one large and harmonious system of free and co-operative labour, general social changes are wanted, changes of the general conditions of society, never to be realised save by the transfer of the organised forces of society, viz., the State power, from capitalists and landlords to the producers themselves.

(c) We recommend to the working men to embark in co-operative production rather than in co-operative stores. The latter touch but the surface of the present economical system, the former attacks its groundwork.

(d) We recommend to all co-operative societies to convert one part of their joint income into a fund for propagating their principles by example as well as by precept, in other words, by promoting the establishment of new co-operative fabrics, as well as by teaching and preaching.

(e) In order to prevent co-operative societies from degenerating into ordinary middle-class joint stock companies (*sociétés par actions*), all workmen employed, whether shareholders or not, ought to share alike. As a mere temporary expedient, we are willing to allow shareholders a low rate of interest.'[7]

Again, at the Brussels Congress of 1868. the International resolved:

'If we are such partisans ... of trade unions ... it is not only from regard to the necessities of the present, but also the future social order. To explain, we do not simply consider these as necessary palliatives (note that we do not say remedies), no, our views are much higher. From the bottom of the chaos and misery in which we struggle, we lift our eyes to a more harmonious and happy society. Then we see in these trades unions the embryos of the great workers' companies which will one day replace the capitalist companies with their thousands of wage-earners, at least in all industries where collective force is used and there is no middle way between wage-slavery and association. (As has been shown by recent strikes, Union funds may be used for setting up co-operative productive societies.)

Yet is must be noted (and this is an important point) that the productive associations to arise from the trades unions will not be the trifling societies that the present day associations are. These latter, excellent, we admit, as example and precept, do not seem to us to have in fact any great social future, any part to play in the renovation of society, for, consisting only of a few individuals, they can only end ... by creating beside the bourgeoisie or third estate, a fourth estate, having beneath it a fifth estate yet more wretched. On the other hand the productive societies arising from the trades unions will embrace whole industries ... thus forming the new corporation ... founded on mutuality and justice and open to all.

...This transformation of trade unions will take place not in one country alone, but in all, or all at least that are at the head of civilisation.'[8]

Marx's own appreciation of the limits of co-operation notwithstanding, his attitude to the burgeoning producer co-operative movement can be very clearly appreciated from the notes he wrote in the margins of Bakunin's book *Statism and Anarchy*, when he answered Bakunin's not unreasonable charge that worker representatives, once separated from their constituents, would 'cease to be workers, and look down on the whole common workers' world from the height of the state.' 'If Mr. Bakunin' wrote Marx 'only knew something about the position of a manager in a workers' co-operative factory, all his dreams of domination would go to the devil.'[9]

On this last point, Marx was at least partly wrong, and his error was carefully, if onesidedly, pointed up by Beatrice Webb, in her pioneering study of co-operation in Great Britain. We shall return to this point. But in general, the movement to establish co-operative factories cannot be evaluated outside the context of the Labour Movement which gives rise to it. If producer co-operatives are part of a wholesale onslaught upon the powers of capital, in a dynamic upsurge of trade union and labour action, then they have a quite different meaning, as stimuli and examples, from that which they may come to acquire in periods of recession in militant labour activity. In the context of modern Britain, new co-operatives raise trade union self-confidence, and stimulate the demand for democratisation of public sector industries at the same time that they undermine the assumption of the inevitable rectitude of managerial prerogatives. If there is no breakthrough on the overall political plane, of course we can have no reason to imagine that the market pressures to which such co-operatives will be exposed will not succeed in eroding their limited independence and autonomy.

The question is not, and cannot be posed as, a problem of class action versus group action. Social classes are composed of groups. If the groups which constitute them lack power, then the classes which align them into an appreciation of their wider interests will also lack power. There are numerous very real differences of interest within social classes, and this is why democratic forms of political organisation are quite irreplaceable, if such tensions are to be regulated to any common advantage, and if conflicts are to become a source of creative development. Of course such groups cannot be encouraged to act outside, or contrary to, common interests: but neither can the *real* interests of any social class be determined without a free play of contending arguments reflecting all the partial interests which actually exist within the wider social context of the class as a whole. Of course, again, the market, which will inevitably corrode and dissolve such islands of industrial democracy as may be isolated within it, determines that the answering socialist strategy must be a plan. But such a plan must either be a voluntary convergence of free associations of producers, or it will be an arbitrary and therefore repressive force.

What enables us to say that the working class *is* a class is the fact that 'objectively' it has a series of over-riding interests which differentiate it from, and oppose it to, other classes. This fact does not in the least annul distinctions, based on differences of interest, within it. Even within a particular factory, workers on the night shift will frequently see their interests as being quite sharply distinct from, and sometimes opposed to, the workers on the day shift. Minor annoyances about the condition in which plant is left can be extremely important from time to time. Such minor annoyances will normally be focused within a wider understanding which persuades night-shift workers that they have every reason to act in a united manner with day-shift workers at the level of trade union organisation in the plant. But the trade union will only be weakened if it attempts to subordinate one shift to the other. Its strength derives from its capacity to provide genuine scope for the resolution of problems and grievances, and for the realisation of the interests of all the divergent sectors which it organises. At the level of the whole economy this also applies.

Ernest Mandel is quite right to point out that workers in the electricity supply industry depend upon workers from the mining industry, and vice versa. This dependence, which integrates everyone employed in modern industry with everyone else, also separates everyone from everyone else on specific questions. The overwhelming need for democracy as the regulator of this ambivalent situation arises precisely from the need to discover a harmonious means for resolving divergent interests within the working class, and for converting the tensions and frictions of intra-class conflict into positive stimuli for social progress. Obviously coal-miners need a voice in the planning of the electricity supply industry: and equally obviously, it is impossible to insist upon such a voice without surrendering equivalent rights to power workers in the determination of mining priorities. But the needs which make this point obvious will themselves persuade the relevant groups of workers to search for means of co-ordinating their efforts and regulating their discussions. No good purpose is served by attempting to discourage group organisation, leave alone forbid it.

Ernest Mandel as a political thinker is very far from that notion of a totalitarian or monolithic political organisation which deformed mainstream modern Marxism for so many decades. But he has not resolved the problem of how to underpin the socialist variant of political pluralism which he seeks to uphold; unless autonomous groups are able to defend their interests against the wider collective if necessary, the democratic process becomes a purely ideal one, with no material foundation. Of course, the hope that such a process could survive in such a disembodied state could legitimately be nourished by many schools of thought, but not by Marxists.

Democratic structures are about regulation by persuasion and change by consent. Without doubt, they still represent an interplay of forces, and they are still prone to make erroneous decisions, when these erroneous decisions are viewed in the light of hindsight. But all the central problems of modern socialist planning have been posed in the absence of effective workers' democracy. Whether one belongs to the school of Preobrazhensky, Guevara (or possibly Mao) or whether one supports the view of Bukharin and so many modern East European communist leaders: in the light of the tragic history of modern socialism, one is bound to appreciate that the fundamental question, far more significant than the priority which is to be given to moral or material incentives, or the speed of advance to socialist forms of distribution, is the question of the democratic regulation of central decision-making. Such regulation is out of the question if the initiative does not rest firmly with workers at the grassroots. In this sense, the notions of Marx, as reflected in the Minutes of the First International, are far more helpful than the subsequent arguments which were developed, sometimes creatively in spite of the odds, by socialist leaders who were able to speak from positions of command in heavily centralised parties and states.

* * *

Within a capitalist society, if there is no early hope of structural transformation, the fate of cooperatives is always fraught with difficulties. The original co-operative idea, as set forward by Vansittart Neale, the pioneer Christian Socialist, was universalist in its scope:

'Theoretically, the idea we endeavoured to spread was the conception of workers as brethren – of work as coming from a brotherhood of men associated for their common benefit – who therefore rejected any notion of competition with each other as inconsistent with the true form of society, and, without formally preaching communism, sought to form industrial establishments communistic in feeling, of which it should be the aim, while paying ordinary wages and interest at the rate I have mentioned, to apply to the profits of the business in ways conducive to the common advantage of the body whose work produced them.'[10]

Of course, as co-operative production was established in labour-intensive industries (in Britain during the 1860s and afterwards), practical considerations of survival in a hostile market came to be more and more oppressive. Beatrice Potter (Webb) provided the most generally known analysis of the fate of the British producer co-operatives which were established in the second half of the 19th century, many of which were directly provoked into existence by industrial disputes, and formed in a hopeful period of high militancy. In 1890 she discerned four classes of co-operative among the surviving organisations:

'Class I. Associations of workers formed on the Christian Socialist model; selecting the committee of management from among their own numbers, and employing members only.
Class II. Associations of workers of like character: but which have bound themselves over to, or had imposed upon them, an irremovable governor or irremovable committee-men.
Class III. Associations of workers governing themselves, but employing outside labour – practically, small masters.
Class IV. Societies in which outside shareholders and stores supply the bulk of capital, but in which the workers are encouraged or obliged to take shares, although they are disqualified from acting on the committee of management.'[11]

Of these the most numerous was the third grouping, from which Beatrice Webb was able to cite a number of entirely undesirable specimens, in whose employment very exploitative conditions prevailed. The second group included four 'comparatively large societies'; in the first group there were only eight societies, four of which were very small. The fourth group included societies which showed a wide variety of different types of constitution, and as a category included the most energetic and successful organisations. But the whole of this group employed only 1,274 workers, and of these only 455 were full members.

On the basis of her studies, which have been cogently questioned since, Beatrice Webb provided a description of what she saw as the most common pattern of co-operative evolution, from idealistic partnership, through capital starvation and intense competition either to bankruptcy or to the adoption of some form of joint stock company status. For this reason she argued that associations of producers are anti-democratic in their structure.

'In the first place, it is a strangely distorted view of democracy to break a community into tiny self-governing circles of producers, which by the very nature of their activities must fight each other to the death or combine to impose price and quality on the public. For it is self-evident that all Associations of Producers, whether they be capitalists buying labour, or labourers buying capital, or a co-partnership between the two, are directly opposed in their interests to the interest of the community. This fundamental opposition can only be counteracted by their rivalry or competition with each other to secure the custom. They are, and must always remain, profit-seekers – intent on securing a large margin between the cost of production and the price given. As profit-seekers they stand constantly in the presence of two contending spirits – the spirit of competition and the spirit of combination. For, to parody the words of a prose poet, "under the influence, first of one, then of the other, they spring from the gamble of competition to the plunder of monopoly, and alight from the plunder of monopoly on the gamble of competition, and know not which is most profitable".'[12]

This archetypal Fabian view has unwittingly come to be accepted as 'marxist' by many marxian spokesmen, whatever Marx himself may have said. It is quite apparent, for instance, how closely Ernest Mandel's argument echoes Beatrice Webb's.

In England producer co-operatives are registered under legislation which had been introduced as a result of the lobby of Christian Socialists in the mid-19th century (the main Act of Parliament, The Industrial & Provident Societies' Act, was passed in 1852, to be followed by additional measures in 1893, 1952, 1961 and 1965. This last Act consolidates all the legislation under which modern co-operatives are registered.) All such registration is quite distinct from registration under the Companies' Act, under which limited liability is provided to public and private companies. By 1900 there were more than 100 of them, the bulk of which were organised in a body known as the Co-operative Productive Federation (CPF). The decline of this Federation has been consistent through this century, and it currently organises something like a score of associations, most of which are very small indeed. The largest producer co-operative in England to be registered under the Industrial & Provident Societies' Acts is a shoe company at Leicester which provides work for 1000 people. Yet, as Derek Jones points out in *The New Worker Co-operatives*, the survival capacity of the small sample covered in this body was favourably comparable with that of similar capitalist concerns, and there is good reason to query some of the Webbs' more caustic judgements.

As we have already explained, none of the newly formed 'co-operatives' has chosen to avail itself of this legislation. In the face of the modern, largely consumer-oriented, co-operative movement, the new organisations tend to maintain a jealous separatism. Certainly, some of the new enterprises are far more dependent upon the trade union movement for support than on any other social network. During a television interview with spokesmen of the IPD Fisher-Bendix co-operative (now renamed Kirkby Manufacturing and Engineering), it became plain that trade unionists in the Liverpool area had been pressing their employers to conclude contracts with the new co-operative, although the spokesmen of the co-operative were understandably reluctant to provide further details of this system of trade organisation.

There is no reason to believe that new co-operatives in Britain would fare any better than the old ones, if their example were not to encourage a wholesale breakthrough in the struggle for industrial democracy, which in British conditions would certainly mean major extensions of nationalisation, and a reversal of the relationships of power within the then greatly diminished private sector. If key parts of the growth centres of the British economy are to be taken under public ownership, with democratic forms of administration, then the co-operatives will undoubtedly find their circumstances transformed.

But if British capitalism weathers its current fierce crisis, and emerges, slimmed and more rapacious, to face a future of decades, then Beatrice Webb's milestones, for all Mr. Jones' reservations about their accuracy, will almost certainly record not only past progress, but also the future of Mr. Benn's brave new experiments in co-operation.

Those socialists who say wryly that it is not possible to build socialism in one factory are, however, very wide of the mark. Of course it is not. It is not possible to build socialism in one country either. But if the social revolution breaks out in one country, one tries to defend it there. And if we can defend a transformation of the power structure within an individual plant, of course we should try to do so. Such a transformation will have far less social consequences for being a partial one: but it will still provide a powerful inducement to thought for people outside its immediate range. The workers' co-operatives at Triumph Meriden, Kirkby, and the *Scottish Daily News* are in the great tradition of a modern revolutionary thinker who 'put up a big-character poster, and called upon the masses to bombard the headquarters': if the masses come, the posters will have succeeded. If they don't, new posters will have to be devised.

First Published in 1976

Footnotes

1. 'Factory Work-ins', by A.J. Mills: *New Society 22* August 1974.
2. See Geoffrey Sheridan's interview with Susan Shapiro *The Guardian* 15.6.1972.
3. *Inside Story*, 'How Red was Briant Colour?' No.10, August 1973.
4. See Bel Mooney, 'The Lessons of Leadgate' *New Statesman* 27.4.1973
5. 20th July 1974.
6. Journal of the International Marxist Group, London, Volume 2, number 3, Winter/Spring 1975.
7. Documents of the First International 1864-6, Volume 1, FLPH, Moscow, 1964, pp.346-7.
8. Cf Raymond Postgate, *Revolution*, Harper Torch books.
9. Marx: *The First International and After,* Pelican Marx Library, pp.336-7.
10. Beatrice Potter, *The Co-operative Movement* Chapter V, p.118
11. Ibid p.139
12. Ibid p.156

13

A Balance Sheet

This chapter was the conclusion of my little book: Work-ins, Sit-ins and Industrial Democracy. *It attempts to draw conclusions from the experiences of work-ins and sit-ins, and to widen the agenda for a more difficult time which was already making itself apparent, with the installation of the Thatcher Government.*

At the same time, rich new experiences needed to be assimilated, most notably the famous Lucas initiative, which was perhaps the most audacious and wide-ranging experiment by the shop stewards' movement.

This essay was published in 1981, by Spokesman Books.

By 1975, although it was showing no signs of abating, the uprush of factory occupations had already established its main practical lessons. At a time when new investment meant displacement of labour on a significant scale, struggles about redundancy were bound to become more prevalent and intractable. That the processes of technological unemployment were to be joined by a structural crisis of British industry, as the weakest and least viable competitor in the advanced capitalist world began visibly to flag, lagging further and further behind in a murderously punishing race, only implied that such struggles would be less and less avoidable.

The first slogans of the UCS occupiers came from old socialist text-books. 'Nationalise', cried almost everyone. Nationalisation was by no means an inappropriate response, and indeed it will almost certainly continue to be widely applied in further response to developing crisis. But nationalisation, to put matters mildly, is by no means a job-saving expedient. The main nationalised industries in post-war Britain have all been arch-rationalisers. Mining production, to take a typical example, has been maintained with a rapidly dwindling labour force, so that a one-time dominant miners' union has long been relegated to the TUC's middle league, its membership having shrunk well below half its postwar expectations, (and all too likely to shrink yet more when modern collieries come into full production at Selby or the Vale of Belvoir: from whence thousands more jobs will then be wasted away in the older coalfields[1]). The streamlining of railways, fierce labour economies in electricity generating, the transformation of gas supply: all these examples of concentration of production with an ever smaller workforce are too well-known to need rehearsing in detail. The more recent sacrifice of the steel industry merely underlines the trend. If any were to doubt such evidence, they need only look to British Leyland: as Michael Barratt Brown has argued, the combined effect of all these labour economies 'has at least equalled the job-destruction of the giant transnational companies in closing their plants in Britain'.[2] Necessary though an extension of conventional forms of public ownership may be, it will surely not provide all the conditions for the recreation of full employment.

As the slump began at first to take hold of the British economy, more and more workers began to look for militant means of defending their jobs, and sit-ins became widespread. This trend has continued even into the acutely adverse times of the Thatcher administration, while more conventional defensive industrial reactions such as strikes or go-slows were becoming extremely difficult to carry through.

In the second half of 1980, when unemployment rose substantially over 2,000,000, the number of work stoppages declined rapidly:

	Number of strikes beginning in month	
	1979	*1980*
July	185	67
August	218	63
September	172	98
October	196	99
November	131	53
December	53	n.a.

	workers involved in strikes in progress in month	
	1979	*1980*
July	662,000	168,000
August	4,103,000	118,000
September	11,716,000	206,000
October	3,508,000	191,000
November	606,000	157,000
December	190,000	n.a.

Source: *Employment Gazette*, December 1980.

But even during this economic blizzard, the mere threat of plant occupations could still sometimes serve to improve offers of compensation for loss of jobs, since managements often wished to avoid the long exposure to critical commentary which, it has been learnt, very commonly accompanies sit-ins or work-ins.

As far as job-protection is concerned, the range of possible demands which could be made by workers was much enriched by the early success of the first handful of producer co-operatives. Here was a form of common ownership which could be carried through on a small scale, which gave the initiative to workpeople themselves, and which did not depend on centralised bureaucratic forms of management. For the micro-sector of the economy this was an option which was bound to prove attractive. Even so, critics were not slow to point out that the new co-ops emerging from work-ins often employed fewer people than had been originally dismissed, while those re-employed commonly accepted modified work practices, which would have been resisted if they had been introduced by a private boss. Often such critics were blind to the similar, but more pronounced, failings of nationalised concerns. Of course, people are willing to pay a price for self-management, once they come to believe it possible. Yet for the collapsing large firms, for derelict old industries, for multinational subsidiaries, such prescriptions have been very difficult to apply, and it is not surprising that they have seldom taken practical effect. That co-operation will grow can hardly be doubted. As unemployment soars towards the three-million level, the task of re-employing so vast an army falls well outside the reach of normal central government initiative. Large manufacturing projects are in any case prone to be capital intensive, so that new jobs each cost a prodigious investment. More: such projects take time to plan and launch, and it is indeed quite common for them to involve a longer span between the drawing board and the first deliveries of actual products than the entire lifetime of a British Parliament. Bureaucratically initiated plans which require from five to seven years in which to bear fruit, while they will be very much needed, will not be enough for any government which seeks the early restoration of full employment.[3]

Of course, public services, especially the personal social services, are commonly labour intensive, and they can absorb a large labour force if only they can be adequately funded. But the continuous displacement of workers by innovative technology in manufacturing industry will ensure that there are strenuous demands for more co-operative and municipal enterprise, as well as for the revival of such welfare services as pre-school education and a functioning health service. Decentralised initiatives will become as important in this process as central state policies, and this may mean innovations which go far beyond the early example of the sit-in movement.

Such stratagems may well come easily to a trade union movement which has been to school with UCS and its responding imitators. There has been a further stimulus to learning in the related experience of the Lucas Aerospace workers, whose combine committee prepared a thousand-page blueprint for conversion to socially useful production when their company was facing the possibility of serious contraction during that brief interlude when it seemed that military spending might be seriously cut back.[4] The Lucas stewards researched areas of potential need in a wide variety of health and social service pressure groups, and also called upon rich resources of inventiveness among the members they represented. Their alternative corporate plan, which has been described in some considerable detail elsewhere, included market-oriented proposals for innovative high technology projects such as the 'power-pack', a device which couples a small internal combustion engine to a stack of batteries in order to provide almost silent motive power at savings of 30% in fuel consumption and 80% in pollution; or for greatly improved heat pumps and advanced wind-generators. It also included a variety of products which might normally be aimed at the caring services, such as kidney machines, which were already manufactured in inadequate numbers by enterprises within the Lucas Group. Mike Cooley, a spokesman of the Lucas Committee, provides a moving report of one of the inventions which the Lucas workpeople pioneered:

> 'Before we even started the corporate plan our members at the Wolverhampton plant visited a centre for children with Spina Bifida and were horrified to see that the only way they could propel themselves about was literally by crawling on the floor. So they designed a vehicle which subsequently became known as Hobcart – it was highly successful and the Spina Bifida Association of Australia wanted to order 2,000 of these. Lucas

would not agree to manufacture these because they said it was incompatible with their product range and at that time the corporate plan was not developed and we were not able to press for this. But the design and development of this product were significant in another sense: Mike Parry Evans, its designer, said that it was one of the most enriching experiences of his life when he actually took the Hobcart down and saw the pleasure on the child's face – it meant more to him, he said, than all the design activity he had been involved in up to then. For the first time in his career *he actually saw the person who was going to use the product that he had designed.* It was enriching also in another sense because he was intimately in contact with a social human problem. He literally had to make a clay mould of the child's back so that the seat would support it properly. It was also fulfilling in that for the first time he was working in the multi-disciplinary team together with a medical type doctor, a physiotherapist and a health visitor. I mention this because it illustrates very graphically that it is untrue to suggest that aerospace technologies are only interested in complex esoteric technical problems. It can be far more enriching for them if they are allowed to relate their technology to really human and social problems.'[5]

There were other numerous creative designs. One was that of the road-rail vehicle, which can drive on rails where these exist, but retract its flanges in order to navigate roads when it reaches them. This vehicle would cut the expenditure involved in developing new railways by a considerable factor, since it would not be necessary to tunnel or drive costly cuttings, because the vehicle could navigate inclines as steep as one in six on its pneumatic tyres. (Conventional railways only function with inclines of not more than 1:80, which means that even before oil-inflation they commonly cost £1 million per track mile.)

The Lucas initiative was originally provoked in a meeting which took place between the shop stewards and Tony Benn whilst he was still Industry Minister. Nonetheless, it encountered sustained passive resistance by the Wilson Government after the 1975 U-turn.[6] Although the Labour Party, as distinct from the government, enthusiastically embraced the alternative plan, government intervention to bring it into force was never forthcoming. The new device of planning agreements was simply not activated, and it was left to others to support this quite extraordinary movement. By the 1980s, the more adventurous local authorities were beginning to be urgently interested in rational projects for job creation, and the search began for forms of local enterprise which could draw upon the Lucas experience.

It is safe to say that events like these have changed the intellectual map of the Labour Movement.

As the issues raised go home in their full force, we begin to see the possibilities for a socialism based upon local initiative, creating new forms of productive association and establishing a new relationship between social planning for community needs and the operation of a changed market. The mental barriers to this development have begun to go down, one after another.

Among the fences which have sagged, sometimes to the point of collapse, has been the once formidable barrier of property as an institution. Property has always been a relationship between people, not, as it has often seemed, a relationship of people to things. But commonly people have seen it upside down, as Marx insisted in the first chapter of *Capital*. He was not the sole originator of this insight. 'The first person', said Rousseau, 'who, having fenced off a plot of ground, took it into his head to say *this is mine* and found people simple enough to believe him, was the true founder of civil society'. That is to say, property consists in thinking of a claim, and persuading one's neighbours to accept it. Once the idea has currency, we are in 'civil society'.

The right to property as exclusive private use had hitherto been justified by different philosophers, either as a right to that with which one's labour had been mixed (the view associated with John Locke) or as an act to ensure the public peace (as Hobbes saw it). Hobbes presumed that before the establishment of the 'sovereign power' all men were equally entitled to all existing natural objects, 'which necessarily causeth war', so that private property was both 'necessary to peace' and dependent on sovereign power for its enforcement, and therefore existence.

For Hegel, who identified the State as the embodiment of Reason, and who saw freedom as existing only within the framework of its laws, this judgement could be simplified into the catchphrase 'property is the first reality of freedom'. For Locke, every man 'has a property in his own person. This nobody has any right to but himself. The Labour of his body, and the work of his hands, we may properly

166

say, are his. Whatsoever, then, he removes out of the state that Nature hath provided and left it in, he hath mixed his Labour with it, and joined it to something that is his own, and thereby makes it his property'.

Doctrines such as these all had powerful liberal implications, (albeit different ones) when small producers were the predominant economic force. But they came, however, to have a radically different meaning as production and ownership were concentrated into ever fewer controlling hands. Marx witnessed this in his youth, when he saw the Prussian Diet busily abolishing the common rights of the peasantry. If property *could* be monopolised, then it *would* be monopolised, he concluded. Liberal philosophers drew similar conclusions more timidly, as when T.H. Green insisted that property had 'become incompatible with its idea' when it began to present an obstacle to free development of the personality rather than a stimulus to such development. If one's freedom to develop one's faculties depends on access to property, and if the prior concentration of ownership prevents such access, then property is now the basis of unfreedom, whatever the philosophers thought before. Over the centuries we have seen an evolution from little watermills with a few dozen employees to transnational companies with greater resources than entire nation states. 'Monopoly' in this sense has become a salient fact of life. Yet attitudes to property have, for a long time, been mixed. Old doctrines have held their force long after they have ceased to be true in any but the most marginal sense. Of course people will defend private property in the marrows or beans grown on their allotments by the persistent application of their own muck and sweat. But this response will not offer them any guarantee of freedom when their interests as employees or citizens run foul of General Motors or the General Electric Company.

A famous survey by Colin Hurry and Associates, in 1959,[7] showed a small but significant majority of Labour voters in 129 marginal constituencies were opposed to any further nationalisation. Labour voters divided 36% to 42% on the issue. The survey was crudely designed and rightly provoked strong criticism at the time: but the adverse vote on nationalisation could not be explained by the huge rationalisation programmes which were subsequently to hit these industries, in the following decade. The result could in part, perhaps, be accounted for because nationalisation was not responsible for any perceptible change in the status and participatory powers of the workers who were directly affected by it: but this would undoubtedly have been a minority judgement, since those wanting greater democratic control would normally seek reform of existing nationalised industries, which was quite compatible with an extension of nationalisation, and, indeed, likely to provoke one. No, there are strong grounds for believing that this kind of reaction represented genuine opposition, which in that time reflected deeply ingrained received attitudes to property.

Such thinking certainly affected the argument in the Labour and trade union movements, and was involved in the background of the debate on the revision of the Labour Party's constitution, in which attempts were made by Hugh Gaitskell and his associates to amend Clause IV, suppressing the Party's commitment to the 'common ownership of the means of production, distribution and exchange'. At the grassroots, one commonly heard arguments in favour of private property which harked back to classical liberal theory. 'How would you like it' one could be asked 'if you worked all your life to build up a shop, and the government came and took it?' Such property rested on the fact that its owner had 'mixed his (or her) labour' with the equipment at issue, and it would easily have been understood by Locke two and a half centuries earlier. It had, however, nothing whatever to do with owning ICI or Rolls Royce, which aggregates combined far more labour than had ever been mixed with anything by their founding fathers, or indeed their succeeding stockholders. Why was it possible to apply it, erroneously, to such different cases? This has been explained, sociologically, by the concept of reference groups. People commonly identify with others like themselves. They compare themselves with their peers, and not with outlandish outsiders. Only some great crisis or trauma will provoke a realistic focus on the implications of outsider behaviour. Normally, next door, or the next workplace, give us our standards of expectation.

When a group of adult students interviewed poor people in a Nottingham slum, they found that many of them defined 'wealth' as a weekly income which was actually below national average earnings, and few thought of it as implying ownership of any assets at all. Those few saw wealth as being 'a house and a car'. Half a million shares in Boots or Players was a thought not only completely outside their daily experience, but beyond any practical imagination.[8]

The 'revisionist' current in the Labour Party was, of course, greatly more sophisticated than this. In *Twentieth Century Socialism*, a classic statement of the arguments of the right-wing grouping, we find three key propositions supporting the view that 'the case for complete common ownership' was misconceived.

'Once the state owns all capital resources, no one but the state is able to take decisions as to their disposal. Every business activity is subservient to the will of the government. There is no freedom to experiment with ideas which have not won state approval. The man who wishes to risk or dare is a misfit – or worse. To eliminate all private capital is to open the road to totalitarianism.

The second misconception lay in the belief that ownership was only dangerous in private hands. Once it had been transferred to public hands – so it was thought – the power it represented would be relatively harmless, for society would control it for social ends. Experience has now shown that the power of ownership, even in public hands, may still be dangerous. It is still open to abuse and the individual has still to struggle to assert his rights in face of it. Ways have to be found to control the powers of ownership, whether they are privately or publicly held.

The third, and perhaps most serious, misconception was the belief that ownership was one indivisible right, which could be held only as a whole – either by private persons or by public authorities; an industry was either wholly in private or in public control. In fact ownership consists of a bundle of rights. These rights are not sacred; they are upheld by the state and society. They are not fixed and unalterable; they can be changed and modified to any degree that state and society desires, and indeed they are constantly changing. Nor are they indivisible. Each separate right can be limited separately and by different methods; some can be in private and some in public hands.

Take, for example, the main rights associated with the ownership of business enterprise. There is the right to decide what is to be produced, the right to retain profits for personal use, the right to dispose of capital assets, the right to hire and fire. None of these rights are now absolute; each may be limited in one way or another. What is produced may be subject to direct government control, or, alternatively, to controls over the equipment or materials which the industry may use. Distributed profits may be curtailed by taxation, or by legislation to limit dividends. Capital transactions may be regulated. The engagement and dismissal of workers may be made to obey conditions agreed with the trade unions. Each right of ownership may in turn be circumscribed or transferred; indeed the rights of ownership can be invaded to such an extent that ownership no longer confers power. Little but the title – and the right to dispose of it – remains.

The twentieth century has witnessed how, step by step, the old unrestricted rights of ownership in regard to labour have been whittled away – through legislation, through trade union organisation, through full employment – with the result that the power relationship between capital and labour today stands transformed even when ownership is still in private hands'.[9]

Arguing only on the plane of the authors of this passage, it is easy to see that they in turn share three misconceptions. They conceive of common ownership as purely state ownership, and the ownership of a unitary state at that. But common ownership includes local, municipal, co-operative and syndicalist possibilities, as well as central state ones. It also includes the possibility of 'arms length' relations with the state, such as those enjoyed by universities, or the BBC, or 'responsible bodies' in adult education, which enjoy government funding, but remain autonomous and self-governing, subject only to certain principles of accountability. There is no *a priori* reason why crudely centralised state ownership must predominate in a common ownership economy.

Secondly, while they are quite right to stress the need to defend individual rights against state institutions, they do not appreciate the potential of democratic control mechanisms to do precisely this, and they miss this crucial arm of socialist strategy because they identify public ownership with rigid, hierarchic public corporations of the type we have inherited from Herbert Morrison, much to our cost and woe.

Thirdly, while they are also right to stress that the bundle of actual rights involved in private ownership is subject to erosion, not only by planning statutes, but also by collective bargaining, they do not appreciate the powerful pressure to concentration, which crystallises great private agglomerates with ample powers to sidestep or even manipulate legislation. If taxation can curtail profits, transfer pricing by multinationals can avoid taxation. We have, since the 1950s, obtained ample evidence of how strictly limited and one-sided is the perception of this foolishly unguarded and optimistic analysis.[10]

And a rich part of this evidence came home to the trade union movement during the work-ins and sit-ins. We need only listen to Jack Spriggs, uncovering the manipulations of the Fisher-Bendix management, to put an entirely different valency on changes in the content of property rights to that proposed as appropriate by the Labour revisionists. Indeed, public involvement in the funding of privately controlled enterprise had actually augmented unaccountable power, rather than restraining it.

When the workers at Plessey began their action, it was in protest at the abuse of former public property by a private concern. At one sit-in after another, millions of public money were inextricably involved in the equation the workers had to unravel. Throughout industry, for several years previously, all new investment had attracted a minimum public subsidy of 20%. Social democracy had reduced itself to a policy of generous public handouts to private interests, without any public control. Creeping state intervention, by the time of the 1970s, had thus made a complete muddle of the frontier between private and public zones of investment, without the slightest degree of public sharing in actual responsibility or power. Even the phenomenal growth of employee pension funds, which resulted from successful legislative intervention and collective bargaining during the years of full employment, had not substantially increased workpeople's collective power. Control of vast funds of employee savings in the most part eluded their 'owners', and decisions on investment were predominantly the prerogative of the corporate rich. Yet the fact remained that large sums of money which were deployed by pension funds and insurance companies were the property of industrially voteless working people. The old property shibboleths, once one had to examine them, became quite insupportable.

More: glued up as property had become, it was quite 'incompatible with its idea' if that idea had anything to do with self-fulfilment for the legions of ordinary wage-slaves. After two decades of consensus in politics, in which 'the main rights associated with the ownership of business enterprise' had been fixed more or less constantly at the point already determined at the time of the *Socialist Union* manifesto,[11] no real transfer of power had thereby ensued. Modest concessions to rights in employment had been legislated, first in redundancy payment provisions, and later in the development of tribunal law. But the first of these in no way enhanced the social power of workpeople in their organisations, while it was specifically designed to increase labour mobility, or the availability of labour power as a resource to be used by capital. In other words, it allowed for personal cash benefits in order the better to uphold collective subordination. The second achieved its main extension as a result of the Heath Government's Industrial Relations Act of 1971, and while it conferred certain (largely inadvertent) benefits on labour, it was accompanied by many other deeply resented curbs on purely defensive trade union powers. The rights vested in ownership have not been absolute, that is true: but they never were. But they do still confer substantial arbitrary power, which was clearly exposed in the succession of crises which provoked one factory occupation after another. It is one thing for Town and Country Planning laws to control random advertising: this is a circumscription of ownership rights, but it, and half a hundred similar limitations, bear not at all on the strategic powers 'to decide what is produced ... to retain profits ... to dispose of capital assets ... to hire and fire'. On the contrary, some sit-ins took place to prevent naked cases of asset stripping, or to insist that social property remain social property, or very commonly to assert elementary claims which were in no way otherwise guaranteed in the early 1970s, all the 'revisionist' tracts of the previous quarter century notwithstanding. Not one of the participants in these actions could accept that 'Little but the title – and the right to dispose of it – remains'. Had such a roseate view been true, their often bitter ordeals of struggle would have been quite unnecessary.

As loyal workmen and women suddenly confronted factory closures, they also confronted the hollowness of the claim that 'the power relationship between labour and capital today stands transformed'. Experience had pronounced a sombre verdict on all such nostrums, and that experience was responsible for the gathering shift of opinion within the Labour Movement, which is still in motion.

On the shoulders of those who fought the battles of UCS, Plessey and KME, a distinguished political philosopher has propounded an interesting new view of property, which opens important perspectives.

'Property', he tells us 'although it must always be an individual right, need not be confined, as liberal theory has confined it, to a right to exclude others from the use or benefit of some thing, but may equally be an individual right not to be excluded by others from the use or benefit of some thing. When property is so understood, the problem of liberal-democratic theory is no longer a problem of putting limits on the property right, but of supplementing the individual right to exclude others by the individual right not to be excluded by others. The latter right may be held to be the one that is most required by the liberal-democratic ethic, and most implied in a liberal concept of the human essence. The right not to be excluded by others may provisionally be stated as the individual right to equal access to the means of labour and/or the means of life.'[12]

This thought, which we owe to C.B. Macpherson, does not in itself solve practical political problems, any more than Locke could posthumously administer the American Union after it had enshrined his outlook in its constitution. But it does open a door to a whole area of political argument, in which the workers of Glasgow, or Liverpool, or London, will doubtless become engaged. In an important sense, they already have. By asserting their right to work, to 'access to the means of labour', these men and women were not appealing for totalitarian controls, censorship, political psychiatry or suppression of personal liberty. All of them rightly took for granted all the established liberal freedoms of speech, assembly, worship, and the press. They were not seeking full-time employment in a Polish state with government-controlled trade unions. If they had any criticisms of democratic institutions, those criticisms would emphasise the need for fuller, not less stringent, accountability and openness.

But they did show, both in their many brilliant individual initiatives and in their courageous joint activities, a burning need for quite new institutions, from which none could be excluded from the means to the fullest moral life available to any. The rebirth of socialism, which is what we are talking about, will be a true renaissance of individual human freedom, if it takes its growth-points from such people as these. Precisely inasmuch as shipbuilders, coal-miners, clerks and engineers are determined to widen the real areas of choice and the material scope for self-fulfilment which are available in their own personal lives, and inasmuch as their combined actions serve these individual goals, the new commonwealth itself begins to come to life.

In Britain, in 1981, three million people will soon be without work. Enterprise is a word which now means inertia and greed. Authority is a widely used synonym for unreasonableness. But private property once meant that 'town air was free air', because the guildsman's scissors or hammers were the basis of his independent livelihood. Now it's transnational companies and wholesale displacement of labour. Words change when people change, and we can join our forces to create a vocabulary in which enterprise becomes in truth a shared effort to improvement and mutual care, and authority is understood as uncoerced admiration for example, and nothing more.

Generations of our forebears, in times when windmills were thought to be sophisticated inventions, could imagine a world in which each might grow in the love, care, and effort of others, and all might take uninhibited delight in the achievements of each. Such Utopian thoughts have been unfashionable in an age of lasers, microchips and revisionism. But they are stirring again, and however troublesome they may be to mediamen and entrepreneurs, the sense they make will become apparent to millions of good people, as they in their turns face the issues which provoked this little book and its innumerable inspirers.

First published in 1981

Footnotes

1. For a discussion of the data on these issues, see Ken Coates: *Ashfield: What Went Wrong?* IWC Pamphlet No.53, 1978 and *Industrial Development and Democratic Planning – The Case of Belvoir*, IWC Pamphlet No.61, 1978.

2. Michael Barratt Brown: *Unemployment and Economic Theory* in *Workers' Control*, No.3, 1981.

3. Already in 1981 many local Labour Parties have begun work on proposals for local enterprise boards to stimulate co-operative and direct municipal production. The London Labour Party is proposing to devote the proceeds of a two penny rate (£40m) to this kind of work. The Sheffield Labour-controlled council has set up a working party with local trade unionists to examine employment-creating possibilities. Various local government groupings have examined the possibility of introducing legislation (as is their right under existing law) to extend their powers in this field.

4. See Ken Coates (editor): *The Right to Useful Work*, Spokesman, 1978, Chapters VIII, IX. Also *Turning Industrial Decline into Expansion*, Interim Report prepared by Lucas Aerospace Confederation Trade Union Committee, February 1979.

5. *The Right to Useful Work*, p.201-2.
6. *Democracy versus the Circumlocution Office* by the Lucas Aerospace Combine Shop Stewards' Committee, IWC Pamphlet No.65, 1979.
7. *Survey of Public Opinion on Nationalisation*, Colin Hurry and Associates, 1959, p.4 at seq.
8. Ken Coates and Richard Silburn: *Poverty, The Forgotten Englishmen*, Penguin, 1981, Chapter 7, also *Beyond the Bulldozer*, Nottingham University, Department of Adult Education, 1980, pp.101-15.
9. Socialist Union (Allan Flanders and Rita Hinden): *Twentieth Century Socialism*, Penguin Books, 1956, pp.125-7.
10. This is lucidly presented by Stuart Holland in *The Socialist Challenge*, Quartet 1975.
11. *Twentieth Century Socialism*, op.cit.
12. C.B. Macpherson: *Property*, Blackwell, 1978, p.201.

*　　*　　*

Conclusion

The downfall of the Callaghan administration followed a period of steadily worsening relationships between the Unions and the Labour Party. Soon after the return of Harold Wilson, numbers of skilled workers had been alienated by the effects of a broadly redistributive incomes policy, introduced in the first days of the 'Social Contract'. Their discontent was registered in a series of strikes in the engineering industry. But the same Social Contract, in its earliest days, gave an advantage to unskilled and relatively lower paid workers, which was not undermined for a year or two. By the time that the members of the Transport and General Workers' Union wished to reject the Contract, overruling their General Secretary, Jack Jones, the Labour Government was actually already facing some strong warning signs, had it only been able to read them.

The warnings culminated in the explosive rebellion of low paid workers which became known as the Winter of Discontent. Strong inflationary pressures, combined with a rigorous freeze on all but minimum wage settlements, were reducing the standards of the poorest workers. Labour votes were thus being lost, first among the most, and then among the least skilled parts of the working population, the best and worst paid employees.

In this context, Mrs. Thatcher won the General Election, and the trade union movement as a whole entered into a period of fierce decline.

Suffusing this, we had the rapid acceleration of large-scale unemployment, which always weakens the bargaining power of Labour. The unemployed already numbered a million when the Conservatives commissioned their advertising campaign, by Saatchi and Saatchi, to say that 'Labour Isn't Working'. But under Mrs. Thatcher's stewardship, these dire statistics first doubled, then trebled.

It was bad weather for trade unions. In 1980, largely because of statistical lags in the recording of numbers, the Trade Union Congress reached its highest membership ever, of twelve million one hundred and seventy two thousand. The Thatcher years registered a continuous and rapid union retreat. By 1990, the number of TUC affiliates was below eight and a half million, and by 1995, it had shrunk below seven million. The figure bobbed up and down around 6.7 million from then onwards, until it fell again in 2002 to 6.68 million.

Of course, membership statistics are a crude instrument for measuring trade union influence, and we have to consider other indicators such as the density of trade union recruitment, if we are to reach a clear understanding of the strength of trade unions. (I looked at this problem in the book which I wrote with Tony Topham, Trade Unions in Britain, *[Fontana Books] which was revised to take account of the Thatcher years up to 1988). The Thatcher onslaught joined to these tribulations a remorseless legislative programme designed to weaken trade unions and remove significant legal protections which had hitherto been deemed to be part of their birthright over many years.*

Small wonder that workers' control began to feel the effects of this blizzard. At first, the IWC did what it could to agitate against mass unemployment, which was systematically underreported. By the early '90s, unemployment as measured by the yardstick of the International Labour Office totalled more than four million in Britain, whilst the official figures still recorded something under three million. But the seminars and conferences in which we presented such evidence as that provided by Dr. John Wells of Cambridge University, or the reports of John Hughes of Ruskin College, were increasingly attended by academics and students, together with political activists, and although a sprinkling of trade union loyalists remained, decisively missing were unemployed people themselves.

The IWC Bulletin continued to agitate actively about this matter until 1983. Conferences continued for longer, deriving a lease of life from the influence of workers' control activities in Local Government and a surge of interest in Local Government plans and job creation activities. As late as 1986,

A Balance Sheet

Michael Barratt Brown formulated the questions for discussion at a seminar in County Hall, London, under the title 'Joint Action for Jobs'. The papers of this seminar were published under the same title, and represented a coming together of old IWC campaigners like Robin Murray, Stephen Bodington, Tony Topham, John Hughes, Stuart Holland and Mike Cooley, with influential Councillors, including Ken Livingstone.

Another symposium on local economic planning was organised for the IWC by Tony Topham. But in time, Local Government was grasped in the same nutcrackers which had enfeebled trade unionism.

At the suggestion of Alex Falconer, a Scottish Member of the European Parliament, I wrote to convenors and deputy convenors of shop stewards over a wide area, to find out whether they would be ready to meet up again under the auspices of the Institute, in the late '80s. There were few takers. The Institute was no longer a living thing.

However, it had, over most of two decades, been an effective and challenging grassroots movement, which paid more than lip service to the initiatives of working people. For this reason, it had an exaggerated reputation in the political classes, who were normally quite isolated, and devoid of active popular support. The business of the IWC was not to preach a received doctrine, but to encourage workers to develop their own ideas about how their lives could be enriched if they were able to take control of their own work, and manage together their collective affairs.

During the tense political upheavals which have followed the eclipse of the Institute for Workers' Control none of the matters which brought about its birth have fundamentally changed. Yes, many workers have been to some extent better educated, and are to some extent cleverer. But even if some of them are richer, their dependence has not abated in the slightest. Their work is still owned by someone else. Its objectives are still determined outside their reach.

Yes, people can still be intimidated by unemployment and poverty. They can still be humiliated by the arrogance of power. But nonetheless, they can still thrill to the challenge of real choices, and to the thoughts of freedom. That is why it is unreasonable to doubt that the rediscovery of trade unionism will be followed, before long, by the rediscovery of workers' control.

In the immediate future, this is likely to take the form of new ideas about democratic management of the social and public services, which are answerable, in the last analysis, to the national democratic polity. But it will also take the form of growing international linkages to match and pace the power of transnational capital in the private sector. It will explore the modalities of co-operation between different trade unions, nurtured in different national cultures and political sectors: and it will seek to relate itself to the democratic possibilities of works' councils organised on a transnational scale.

There will be many other books written to explore these issues. But I think that some of them will recognise their kinship with the struggles of an earlier generation, some of whose efforts are recorded here.

Afterword

One of the most important unresolved problems posed by the IWC and all those groups which it inspired concerns the question of the relationship between property and industrial democracy.

It is interesting to note that Neil Kinnock, campaigning for election as Leader of the Labour Party in 1983, told its journal, New Socialist, *that prominent among his allegiances was membership of 'the Institute for Workers' Control'. A little earlier, interviewed by* Marxism Today, *he had informed Sam Aaronovitch, who had asked about Labour's lack of an ideology: 'I happen to think we do have an ideology. It is in Clause IV.'*

The earliest years of Kinnock's leadership saw the repetition of this mantra on all sides. One prominent faction gave itself the name Clause IV, and a number of subsequent frontbenchers cut their teeth in its service.

Indeed, in October 1994, the sudden proposal for its abolition by Tony Blair, newly elected as Leader after the death of John Smith, was so surprising that at first many members did not understand his drift. At the end of his conference oration, he said:

> *'No more ditching. No more dumping. Stop saying what we don't mean. And start saying what we do mean, what we stand by, what we stand for.*
>
> *It is time we had a clear, up-to-date statement of the objects and objectives of our Party...'*

This was a total surprise because it ran completely contrary to the Leader's own statement a few months earlier, when he was interviewed by David Frost during the election campaign for John Smith's successor...

David Frost: *If there was a move to get rid of Clause Four, would you actively oppose that?*

Tony Blair: *I think the most important thing is for the Labour Party to state what its economic priorities are, and there has been discussion about Clause Four over the past couple of years, and I understand why that is, but I think the most important thing at the present time, and I think where everybody in the Party wants to see the Labour Party go, is to construct its policies for the next General Election and make those clear before the British people.*

DF: Do you have your own view on Clause Four? Would you oppose its being dropped?

TB: Well, I don't think that anyone actually wants that to be the priority of the Labour Party at the moment. I mean, I understand why people have raised this, and there are people who have raised it across a whole spectrum of the political party.

DF: Jack Straw, Neil Kinnock...

TB: Absolutely right. But I don't think that anyone is saying now, looking ahead to the next two years in the run-up to an election, that this is what we should focus on. And I think for the vast majority of British people, I don't think they sit out there and debate the intricacies of the Labour Party constitution.

After a perfunctory debate, the old constitution of the Labour Party was unceremoniously annulled and Common Ownership found itself, together with industrial democracy, among those relics least esteemed by New Labour. By 2003, some years into the New Labour renaissance, almost all the most important trade unions have found that the practice of the Blair administration pays little heed to them, and offers results that leave a very great deal to be desired.

But the renewal of the Labour Party must surely presuppose a socialist renewal, a recovery of belief, without which political struggle becomes only an empty war of faction, in pursuit of office without conscience...This contribution to the debate on Clause Four was published in Common Ownership *in 1995. It is excerpted from Chapter 3.*

Introducing their new statement on 'Labour's Objects: Socialist Values in the Modern World', the Blair leadership team offer us a preliminary statement which tells us that 'the Labour Party is a democratic socialist party'. This goes on to offer a menu which could be presented by almost any Liberal:

'It is founded on the simple belief that individuals prosper when supported by a strong and active society, and that people owe a duty to each other as well as themselves. It is from this central belief that our core values are derived: social justice, freedom, opportunity, equality, democracy and solidarity. Democratic socialism sees economic efficiency and social justice as complementary to one another, not opposites; and links together action to establish a prosperous and strong economy with action to attack poverty, increase employment, counter discrimination, curb unaccountable power, and protect the environment.'

What is wrong with such a liberal prospectus? Certainly most of the objects appeal to elementary commonsense. Why is that insufficient?

If democratic socialism 'sees economic efficiency and social justice as complementary to one another, not opposites', what measures does it propose to ensure that its vision begins to correspond to reality? Left alone, economic efficiency as it is conventionally understood stands in no relation whatever to social justice because it is not driven by either law or compassion, but by competition for growth and survival. Aneurin Bevan once summed it up with admirable economy:

> 'What are the most worthy objects on which to spend surplus productive capacity? ... After providing for the kind of life we have been leading as a social aggregate, there is an increment left over that we can use as we wish. What would we like to do with it?
>
> Now the first thing to notice is that in a competitive society this question is never asked. It is not a public question at all. It cannot be publicly asked with any advantage because it is not capable of a public decision which can be carried out. Therefore in this most vital sphere, the shaping of the kind of future we would like to lead, we are disfranchised at the very outset. We are unable to discuss it because the disposal of the economic surplus is not ours to command... The surplus is merely a figure of speech. Its reality consists of a million and one surpluses in the possession of as many individuals... If we reduce the question to the realm where we have brought it, that is to say, to the individual possessor of the surplus, the economist will provide us with a ready answer. He will tell us that the surplus owner will invest it in the goods for which he thinks there will be a profitable sale. The choice will lie with those able to buy the goods the owner of the surplus will proceed to produce. This means that those who have been most successful for the time being, the money owners, will in the sum of their individual decisions determine the character of the economy of the future...But...the kind of society which emerges from the sum of individual choices is not one which commends itself to the generality of men and women. It must be borne in mind that the successful were not choosing a type of society. They were only deciding what they thought could be bought and sold profitably.' *(In Place of Fear)*

That is to say, social priorities, including social justice, *cannot* be assured simply by reliance on the market. This possesses no self-corrective mechanism for transferring individual surpluses 'to attack poverty, increase employment, counter discrimination, curb unaccountable power, and protect the environment'.

'Justice' has to be *outside* the market, and presupposes a capacity by the public authority to override it. But the market has been systematically eroding and dissolving all external pressures to regulate or control its operations for many years. In this respect it has enjoyed very considerable success.

In the past, action for correction could be taken, not by the market, but by government. In pursuit of these social goals, government might, by taxing profits and high incomes, transfer the revenue so garnered to good redistributive effect. But the Labour Party's present front bench insists that it proposes no structural shift in taxation other than the blocking of 'loopholes'.

Unfortunately, the main 'loophole' which frustrates the tax inspector is the device of transfer pricing, which is systematically deployed by multinational corporations to transfer their profits from wherever they may have been earned, to the most beneficial area: from the point of view of tax advantages, amongst other things. Of course, transnational corporations also have to devote a lot of attention to speculation in the currency markets, in order to stay ahead in the game of competitive devaluation, which was so strongly boosted when the British Government fell out of the Exchange Rate Mechanism on Black Wednesday, September 16th, 1992. National tax inspectors all around the world chorus their lamentations about the insurmountable difficulties which are involved in imposing effective taxation on multinational capital. If it could be done, no doubt it would be difficult. But by what other magic does our Leader propose to transfer the profits of the growth sector of multinational capital, to the socially valid purpose of creating jobs, for instance?

We have lived through a decade and a half in which a wide variety of constraints on the free operation of markets have been removed...

But someone wins. The winners acquire monopoly powers over whole products and industries, and dominate all the people in them. Before he was elected in 1964, Harold Wilson told us:

> 'At every level of our national life, talent and ability are wasted; our children do not get equal opportunities or our citizens equal chances to develop their qualities and energies. In an age of great potential plenty, we are still in this country cursed by indefensible pockets of shameful poverty and injustice which twelve years of so-called affluence have not removed.'

Today, the poverty no longer lives in pockets, but blankets large sections of a society which subsists in profound social crisis. To tell us that growth on its own will facilitate action for improvement is plainly not true. Perhaps growth *could* enable action to be taken, but the mechanics of such action, here, are all-important. Normally, growth will aggravate the problem. There is no such thing as 'trickle down' in the field of wealth. Wealth is energetically hoovered up. What trickles down is misery, poverty, rejection and destitution.

Today most Liberals deny this, but this was not always the case. Precisely at the time when Clause IV was written, to separate the Labour Party from the paternal influence of the Liberals, there were Liberals who were able to see these truths quite plainly. Today, all these intellectual processes have gone into reverse. The most brutal forms of liberalism were espoused by Mrs Thatcher, and imposed with manic zeal. Her single-minded devotion has pulled behind her, first, middle liberal opinion, and now, a significant part of the Labour leadership, whose hunger for office is commendably strong: but unfortunately outweighs any allegiance to its abandoned constituencies.

The new leadership statement has achieved on paper something that generations of supporters of Clause IV have never dreamt of. It has abolished capitalism. Nowhere can this dread concept be found in the new text. The text is so full of reach-me-down values that it might have been composed by Patience Strong, but for the unfortunate fact that it does not rhyme. 'The process of constitutional revision', say the authors, 'is intended to set out our identity as a Party in our own terms for our own age'. But has capitalism really disappeared in this age of comforting and empty froth? It is true that capital has become more fluid, more mobile. At the touch of a button, millions can travel along the wires, or along the optical fibres, to disappear here and materialise in another place. Along the wires, routine tasks are transferred to low-paid Indian women, who programme the bookings for European airlines, and flash the resultant effort back in seconds. Then the prosperous stockholders can board their planes. Reality has not disappeared, but it has been beautifully concealed. Has Tony Blair got access to some of these computer buttons? Will the wires transmit his commands? And will they deliver social justice on all the screens that matter?

Alas, no. The present Labour leadership resembles nothing more than the inhabitants of those South Sea Islands which initiated the cargo cults. Observing that the missionaries who came among them lived very happy lives, the indigenous peoples made a close study of the causes of this happiness. They perceived that the missionaries wanted for nothing, and that the secret of their prosperity lay in the cargoes which were ferried to them in small aeroplanes, at regular intervals. In the cargo, there was nourishment and uplift. Commentaries on scripture and crates of gin brought consolation to the foreign teachers.

Having scientific minds, the natives were quick to agree that the benefits of cargoes might with profit be more widely shared among the excluded. They gathered their forces, and cleared space in the forests, where the planes could land. They lit beacons, to guide them in. And they waited. But no cargoes came.

The long-suffering people of Britain do not have so long to wait. No cargoes are coming. Unless remedial action is taken to redistribute wealth, the poor will decline into even deeper misery. And unless a strong public force generates local enterprise, stimulates co-operation, and encourages common effort, capitalism will assiduously ensure the continuation of present trends. More polarisation, richer rich, poorer poor. These processes will continue with a Queen or without one, with hereditary Peers, or without them, and throughout whatever cosmetic changes might be made to keep hidden the realities of economic power. Is that the modern age, or isn't it?

*　　*　　*

The history presented in the draft document is, to say the least of it, eccentric. It correctly informs us that the first draft of Clause IV appeared in October 1917, the very month of the Bolshevik Revolution. But it goes on to tell us that central planning 'had after all helped Britain to win the war'. Not in October 1917 it hadn't. Neither in 1917 had the Russian Soviets established public ownership and central planning. Their first task, under a variety of forms of workers' control, was to re-establish any kind of production, with or without the help of experienced managers. In 1917 and early 1918, the

184

current of thought that constituted a perceived threat to the Labour leadership was syndicalist, and it seemed threatening because it advocated workers' control in British factories and industries, not in those of Russia or elsewhere.

The preliminary draft for the Clause had been written by Arthur Henderson. It spoke about taking into public ownership 'the monopolies'. This was a long-standing commitment of Henderson's, and it was based, not on socialist doctrine, but on impeccable Victorian liberal teaching. In the philosophical writings of T.H. Green, it had been pointed out that the Hegelian justification of property as 'the first reality of freedom' could no longer be invoked if property was monopolised. This is an old argument, which goes back a long way in political theory. Certainly Marx had identified the same problem that Green treated decades later. Locke had insisted, by contrast, that property was justified where men had 'mixed their labour' with the gifts of nature. But this, too, hit a problem with monopoly. What could happen when all the land was occupied, and none was left vacant to be mixed with the labour of any newcomer? This was the great fascination of America, as a seemingly inexhaustible source of virgin land, in which work would generate property, and thus in Hegelian terms, freedom. But monopoly closed out newcomers, bolted the door against them. From guaranteeing freedom, such property had become inimical to it. Thus, Henderson's formula was a direct echo of more than one important strand of liberal thinking. But Webb's amended version of Clause IV cut that link.

Webb was drawing on the experience of trade unionism during the First World War, and the growth of collectivist responses.

For many workers, the years of the war marked their first experience of something approaching humane working conditions. Employers became more than willing to strike reasonable bargains with their workpeople, because many of them were now remunerated on a 'cost-plus' system which guaranteed all munitions manufacturers a fixed rate of profit over and above the costs they incurred in production. Higher wages were simply higher costs, and offered no detriment to the 'plus' which would be allocated to profits.

Of course the founding fathers lived always in an ambivalent relationship to Liberalism. They were deeply engaged in the commitment to individual freedom, and to the need to create scope for all to become whatever each had it in himself or herself to be. But personal advance, for most, already depended on collective betterment.

Why did Webb's wording prevail? It was precisely attuned to the trade union experience of collective advance in this kind of planned war economy, and it was finely calculated to separate trade union voters from any residual allegiance they might feel to the Liberals as a Party. Since the working class electorate was considerably enlarged in 1918, this was a crucial strategic move.

If Clause IV served to demarcate Labour from the Liberal Party in 1918, what would its removal signify in 1995? Evidently it would mean realignment, in which liberals of either the Liberal or Conservative Parties might feel free to participate.* How participate? By voting? By supporting?

By joining in a common Party? By forming a common government? And what might the programme of such a government be? Who would represent the unemployed, the excluded, the poor, in such an enterprise? What mechanisms would exist to aid these groups of people? And who could represent the other employees? How many of them should be nudged downwards below the poverty barrier?

Capitalism may have become invisible behind its apparatus of wires and high-tech communication. It may no longer have its national roots. It has certainly disappeared from the programme of 'New Labour', which never comes near to mentioning it. But until it is displaced from its authority over our economic life, it will still call all the tunes.

The historical section of the leadership statement tells us that Clause IV was agreed because 'there was genuine revulsion at the sheer anarchy and exploitation associated with the free market of Victorian capitalism'. And the anarchy of modern global capitalism? The destruction of large parts of the world economy, mass starvation

*All this has been justified in the name of Antonio Gramsci as a recipe *for* the creation of what is unappealingly described as a 'hegemonic bloc'. Poor Gramsci is revolving in his grave. It is strange to see this most principled and democratic of all Western communists pressed into service by the most unprincipled and manipulative of all opportunists.

and civil war in former colonies across Africa, and here at home seven and a half million *long-term* unemployed in the territories of the European Community alone: is there no anarchy and exploitation there? Large tracts of Britain are crumbling into physical and moral ruins. Do we need to do sums to explain this?

Nobody, but nobody, in the Labour Movement, will seek to hamper any Labour leadership, if it will tell us how it will restore hope to the forgotten people of Britain, and join forces with others to help the destitute in Africa and elsewhere. A programme for this kind of action could conceivably be an 'adequate expression of what the Labour Party stands for'. But such an expression will not only mention the word capitalism. It will try to analyse what has happened to capital, and seek to find appropriate ways to curtail the immense concentrations of power which it has secreted.

First published in 1995

* * *

Clause IV

Sidney Webb

This article was written for The Observer, *to explain the thinking behind Sidney Webb's proposals for a new constitution for the Labour Party. It was published in 1917. The constitution was adopted the following year.*

The proposal to re-organise the Labour Party, formulated by its National Executive, and circulated to its constituent societies for their consideration, may well prove an event of far-reaching political importance. Instead of a sectional and somewhat narrow group, what is aimed at is now a national party, open to anyone of the 16,000,000 electors agreeing with the party programme.

More important, however, than any of these changes in the constitution is the change of spirit that has inspired them. The Labour Party, which has never been formally restricted to manual-working wage-earners, is now to be publicly thrown open to all workers 'by hand or by brain'.

Its declared object is to be, not merely the improvement of the conditions of the wage-earner, but 'to secure for the producers, by hand or by brain, the full fruits of their industry and the most equitable distribution thereof that may be possible upon the basis of the common ownership of the means of production, and the best obtainable system of popular administration and control of each industry or service'.*

The only persons to be excluded (and that, of course, only by inference) are the unoccupied and unproductive recipients of rents and dividends – the so-called 'idle rich' – whom it is interesting to find *The Times* editorially declaring to be of no use to the community.

The Labour Party of the future, in short, is to be a party of the producers, whether manual workers or brain workers, associated against the private owners of land and capital as such.

Its policy of 'common ownership' brings it, as a similar evolution brought John Stuart Mill – to use his own words in the *Autobiography* – 'decidedly under the general designation of Socialist.'

But it is a Socialism which is no more specific than a definite repudiation of the individualism that characterised all the political parties of the past generation and that still dominates the House of Commons.

This declaration of the Labour Party leaves it open to choose from time to time whatever forms of common ownership from the co-operative store to the nationalised railway, and whatever forms of popular administration and control of industry, from national guilds to ministries of employment and municipal management, may, in particular cases, commend themselves.

What the Labour Party at present means by its Socialism is revealed in the remarkable pamphlet which it has published on its 'After the War Programme', setting forth in a dozen detailed resolutions passed at the Manchester Party Conference exactly what it wishes done with the railways, the canals, the coal mines, the banking system, the demobilisation of the army and munition workers, the necessary rehousing of the people, the measures to be taken for preventing the occurrence of unemployment, the improvement of agriculture, the

*Historical Note: The words 'distribution and exchange' were added to Clause IV of the Labour Party constitution in 1929. They were moved as amendments to the constitution by the Bristol Labour Party and went through without any debate.

taxation to be imposed to pay for the war, the reform of our educational system, and what not.

Opinions will naturally differ as to some of these sweeping proposals, but no one of any education can safely denounce them as unpractical or despise them as ill-informed.

It is, indeed, one of the claims of the Labour Party that science is on their side; that it is their proposals, not those of the Liberals or those of the Unionists, that nowadays receive the general support of the 'orthodox' economists; and that, as a matter of fact, it is essentially their proposals to which every Minister of State, when he is brought up against a difficult problem of administration, has actually to turn – and then to lose his nerve, emasculate what would have got over his difficulties, and produce an abortion which has the advantages neither of individualism nor of collectivism!

But the programme of the Labour Party is, and will probably remain, less important (except for educating the political leaders of other parties) than the spirit underlying the programme, that spirit which gives any party its soul.

The Labour Party stands essentially for revolt against the inequality of circumstance that degrades and brutalises and disgraces our civilisation.

It abhors and repudiates the unscientific and immoral doctrine that the competitive struggle for the means of life is, in human society, either inevitable or requisite for the survival of the fittest; it declares, indeed, in full accord with science, that competition produces degradation and death, whilst it is conscious and deliberate co-operation which is productive of life and progress.

It is unreservedly democratic in its conviction – here also fortified by political science – that only by the widest possible participation in power and the most generally spread consciousness of consent can any civilised community attain either its fullest life or its utmost efficiency. But it recognises that no mere rightness of aspiration or morality or purpose can in themselves accomplish their ends; and that for the achievement of results knowledge and the application of the scientific method is required, notably in the science of society, for the further study and endowment of which it presses.

And finally the Labour Party has faith in internationalism (as distinguished from the characteristically liberal cosmopolitanism). It repudiates all 'Imperialism' or desire for domination over other races. It pleads for the right of each people to live its own life, and make its own specific contribution to the world in its own way, recognising, indeed, no one 'superior race' but 'reciprocal superiorities' among all races.

It is not without significance that the National Executive of the Labour Party has included, as a fundamental object of the party, the establishment of a Federation or League of Nations for such international legislation as may prove possible. No other political party has yet nailed this flag to its mast.

The Labour Party is, without doubt, today the party of inspiration and promise. Tomorrow it may well prove to be the party of the future, destined, perhaps, to play as large a part in the political history of the twentieth century as the Liberal Party did in that of the nineteenth.

The Formation of the Transport and General Workers Union - 1870 - 1922

THE MAKING OF THE LABOUR MOVEMENT

by Ken Coates & Tony Topham

"Should be read by all who wish to see a revitalised trade union and labour movement..." **Jack Jones**

In the last years of the nineteenth century a revolution took place in Britain. The excluded people of our great cities suddenly began to band together. The unskilled workers of London reached out to one another, and as they started to develop their first faltering organisations, they began the transformation of some of the poorest people in Victorian Britain from a mob into a movement.

This authoritative and comprehensive history tells a compelling story, and more. It shows how trade unions created permanent organisation, based on 'recognition' as a key concept. Those who had formerly been excluded or ignored by society now recognised their own strength in association.

The organisation of the unskilled, and the expression of their political and industrial voices, is followed from the struggle for the 'dockers' tanner' in 1889, to Ernest Bevin's passionate advocacy on behalf of the dockers, in 1920. the key figures who shaped events both nationally and regionally are all original thinkers, and are here allowed, whenever possible, to speak in their own voices.

Based on much previously unknown material discovered in the union's own archive in Transport House, this book creates for the first time a total picture of new unionism's emergence, and the parallel emergence of a specifically *Labour* movement. This national movement is shown in all its regional diversity, drawing on its strength from local roots in Britain's ports and urban centres.

"I was never bored, always carried on by the drive of the narrative." Walt Greendale

"**The book shows** how TGWU origins lie deep in Labour history and class development in our country. Indeed, part of the title of this work tries to capture the point that the emergence of the TGWU has been central to the whole character of the British Labour movement and its socialist aspirations." **Ron Todd, former General Secretary.**

"... breathlessly exciting from first to last; ... almost unique." *New Statesman.*

"This marvellous feast is the story about the sinews of the Labour movement." Geoffrey Goodman. *Tribune.*

"I cannot remember when I enjoyed social (or socialist) history so much... " Diana Warwick, *The Guardian.*

"... foremost example of living trade union history. It evokes all the feelings of those times." Mick McGahey, former Vice President, *NUM*

"... a very good read." Financial Times

"... a superb volume ... will strengthen trade unionism everywhere." Jim Mortimer, Former General Secretary, the Labour Party, first Chair ACAS

"What they have to day is of such value that it will be thumbed over by historian for many years to come." Lewis Minkin, European Labour Forum